James Jeffrey

The Gospel of Paul

The Gospel of Jesus

James Jeffrey

The Gospel of Paul
The Gospel of Jesus

ISBN/EAN: 9783337279271

Printed in Europe, USA, Canada, Australia, Japan

Cover: Foto ©Lupo / pixelio.de

More available books at **www.hansebooks.com**

THE GOSPEL OF PAUL
THE GOSPEL OF JESUS

BY

JAMES JEFFREY, M.A.

OF TRINITY UNITED PRESBYTERIAN CHURCH,
POLLOKSHIELDS

AUTHOR OF "THE PERSONAL MINISTRY OF THE
SON OF MAN"

PUBLISHED BY
OLIPHANT, ANDERSON AND FERRIER
EDINBURGH AND LONDON
1899

FOREWORD

THE object of this little work is to present in a popular form the teaching of the Apostle Paul with regard to the Life and Work of Jesus Christ, what he calls "his gospel," and to show how it harmonises with the teaching of Christ and His Apostles. While the cry of our day, "Back to Christ," has led to a more profound study of the words of Christ, it has to some extent tended to depreciate the teaching of Paul. It is true the Saviour does not dwell at length on His atoning death, but we can understand His silence when we remember the unwillingness of His hearers to listen to anything He had to say about His death. It must also be borne in mind that Paul claimed to have received his gospel from Christ Himself. What I have tried to do is to trace the gospel as presented by Paul in his Epistles. I have added three papers on the Epistle to the Hebrews and the General Epistles of Peter and John to exhibit the agreement between the teaching of the great Apostle and those who were the immediate disciples of the Saviour, or who represented the current teaching about the person and work of Christ.

The Rev. P. Rutherford and Rev. William Young, M.A., of Glasgow, have assisted me with the proof-sheets, and to them my grateful thanks are due.

CONTENTS

	PAGE
I. INTRODUCTION	9
II. THE GOSPEL IN THE EPISTLES TO THE THESSALONIANS	15
III. THE GOSPEL IN THE EPISTLES TO THE CORINTHIANS	27
IV. THE GOSPEL IN THE EPISTLE TO THE GALATIANS	38
V. THE GOSPEL IN THE EPISTLE TO THE ROMANS	50
VI. THE GOSPEL IN THE EPISTLE TO THE PHILIPPIANS	62
VII. THE GOSPEL IN THE EPISTLE TO THE COLOSSIANS	73
VIII. THE GOSPEL IN THE EPISTLE TO THE EPHESIANS	84
IX. THE GOSPEL IN THE EPISTLES TO TIMOTHY	95
X. THE GOSPEL IN THE EPISTLE TO TITUS	106
XI. THE GOSPEL IN THE EPISTLE TO THE HEBREWS	116
XII. THE GOSPEL IN THE EPISTLES OF PETER	126
XIII. THE GOSPEL IN THE EPISTLES OF JOHN	136
XIV. SUMMARY OF PAUL'S GOSPEL	146

THE GOSPEL OF PAUL
THE GOSPEL OF JESUS

I

INTRODUCTION

THE prevailing conceptions of the gospel have no doubt been largely determined by the writings of the Apostle Paul. The statements of the Saviour regarding His own person and work, plain and pregnant as these are, run into a peculiar and definite mould when passing through the mind of Paul, and come forth stamped with his own individuality. In more recent times some critics have endeavoured to make out that the writings of the great Apostle set forth a different gospel from that contained in the sayings of Jesus as recorded in the Synoptic Gospels. We recognise the profound truth of Peter's words, "Lord, to whom shall we go? Thou hast the words of eternal life." But it does not follow that the same Spirit of Truth who spake in and through Jesus Christ (Heb. ii. 4) does not speak in and through Paul. Jesus distinctly assured His disciples that He had not spoken the last word or summed up the whole truth to them, and that the Holy Spirit who was to come after His departure would reveal to them new and fuller developments of the truths taught by Himself. He contented Himself with the simplest statements as to His death, statements most unwelcome to His disciples, the explanation of which was left to the future when their minds were opened to understand their Master's words.

It becomes then an interesting inquiry, From what source did the Apostle Paul derive his views of the gospel? Who was his teacher in the knowledge of Christ? What were the influences that coloured his conception of Christian truth? His own answer is clear and explicit. Writing to the Galatians, he says: "For I make known to you, brethren, as touching the gospel which was preached by me, that it is not after man. For neither did I receive it from man, nor was I taught it, but it came to me through revelation of Jesus Christ" (Gal. i. 11, 12); and he adds: "But when it was the good pleasure of God, who separated me, even from my mother's womb, and called me through His grace, to reveal His Son in me, that I might preach Him among the Gentiles; immediately I conferred not with flesh and blood: neither went I up to Jerusalem to them which were apostles before me: but I went away into Arabia" (Gal. i. 15–17). When delivering to the Corinthian Church the simple form for the observance for the Lord's Supper, he rests his teaching on the direct authority of Jesus Himself: "I received of the Lord that which also I delivered unto you" (I. Cor. xi. 23). His epitome of his gospel, presented to the same Church under the form of a short creed, is introduced with these words: "I delivered unto you first of all that which I also received" (I. Cor. xv. 3), the natural inference being that he received it from the Lord, although it has been argued that the absence of the words ἀπὸ τοῦ Κυρίου in the latter passage is emphatic, and affirms the human source of his knowledge.[1] Having frequently to defend his claim to speak with authority, he never hesitates to trace his knowledge to divine revelation. "For this cause I Paul, the prisoner of Jesus Christ in behalf of you Gentiles,—if so be that ye have heard of the dispensation of that grace of God which was given me to you-ward; how that by revelation was made known unto me the mystery, as I wrote unto you in few words, whereby, when ye read, ye can perceive my understanding in the mystery of Christ" (Eph. iii. 1–4).

How, then, was this knowledge communicated to the Apostle? He could not have been wholly ignorant of the facts of the Saviour's life. It is quite possible that he was in Jerusalem at the time of the condemnation and death of Jesus, and he must have known the popular tradition regarding Jesus of Nazareth. The memorable appearances of Stephen in the synagogue of the Cilicians must

[1] *Expositor*, Third Series, x. p. 408.

have made him familiar with the Christian view of Jesus. Are we then to suppose that the risen Saviour communicated directly to the Apostle the facts of His own life and death and the import of His teaching? or are we to take the more natural view that during his retirement, as he meditated on the life and teaching of Jesus, the Holy Spirit led him into that fuller understanding of its meaning, which appears in his writings? There is much to be said in support of the latter view, which is confirmed by Christian experience. The miracle of Paul's conversion remains. What a revelation of Jesus that was to him! What a wonderful opening of the eyes of his understanding! And as the Spirit, acting through his own mind, led him into all the truth we begin to understand the light in which the Crucified appeared to him and the form in which the truth crystallised in his thought. His gospel was not the product of apostolical training. It was the direct outcome of a powerful and original mind, directed in much thoughtful meditation by the Spirit of God. No doubt he learned much from Barnabas, no doubt his close intimacy with Luke, no doubt his intercourse with Peter and John tended to increase his knowledge of the Saviour's life, but his conception of the gospel was formed in those earlier hours when he was alone with the Master and his understanding was enlightened by the Spirit of grace.[1] At the

[1] "The Christ of Paul, in a word, is the Christ of his experience, Christ interpreted to him by his vivid consciousness of the

same time we can trace a distinct development in his view of the gospel. He grew in his knowledge of Christ, as he so often prayed that his converts might do. His presentation of the gospel varied according to the circumstances of those whom he was addressing, at one time simple in the extreme, at another more profound, but the germ of his teaching is the same in his more elaborate writings as it was in his earliest addresses, and this, he declared, he received not from man, but by the revelation of Jesus Christ. The Tübingen school has sought to prove that the teaching of the Pauline Epistles is antagonistic to that of Peter and the other Apostles; but the more carefully the Epistles of Peter and John are examined the more marked is their agreement with the gospel as it appears in the writings of the Apostle Paul.

What, then, was the gospel Paul preached, "My gospel" as he calls it, of which he was not ashamed, because it was the power of God unto salvation? I propose to answer this question by briefly examining the passages in the Epistles bearing his name, which contain his presentation of the gospel of Christ.[1]

divine life which He had given to him. His Christology is the account of that experience in terms suggested by that and reflected in it" (Dr. Somerville, *St. Paul's Conception of Christ*, p. 15).

[1] It is outside of the scope of this little work to discuss the question of the genuineness of the Epistles that bear Paul's name. Besides the four generally received Pauline Epistles, so much is to be said for the genuineness of the others, that I have included them in the documents, which contribute to the understanding of Paul's gospel.

These Epistles are commonly divided into four groups. The first includes the two Epistles to the Thessalonians, written during his second missionary journey, probably between 54 and 56 A.D. The second, known as the controversial Epistles, includes the two Epistles to the Corinthians, the letter to the Galatian Churches, and the Epistle to the Romans, written during his third missionary journey, probably about the year 57 or 58 A.D. The third, known as the prison Epistles, written during his two years' imprisonment at Rome, probably about 61 or 62 A.D., includes the Epistles to the Colossians, Philemon, and Ephesians. The fourth, composed in the interval between his first and second imprisonments, probably about 63 or 64 A.D., includes First and Second Timothy and the Epistle to Titus.

These four groups of Epistles, along with the addresses of the great Apostle recorded by the author of the Acts of the Apostles, contain the gospel Paul was in the habit of proclaiming by word or letter. The burden of his message was always the same, the salvation of men by the death of Christ, meaning by that, not merely their redemption from the curse of sin, but their deliverance from its power and their perfect conformity to the image of God. Salvation with Paul meant a new creation in Christ Jesus.

II

THE GOSPEL IN THE EPISTLES TO THE THESSALONIANS

A NEW era in the development of Christianity began when Paul set foot on the shores of Europe. His arrival in Macedonia was well timed. Men and women were tired of the superstitions of the past. Many of them were ready to welcome any guide who could assist a struggling humanity to attain to a higher and better life, and inspire it with hope in the future. Philippi was the first to receive the new teaching, and there the first Christian Church in Europe was founded. The members of that Church held a high place in the heart of Paul. He could never forget their eager reception of his message, their kindness to himself, or the manner in which they sought to undo the effects of his cruel treatment by the officers of justice in their city. Many a gift did the Apostle receive from them, most opportune in enabling him to prosecute his labours in other cities with greater freedom and independence. From Philippi Paul travelled by one of the loveliest roads in Greece, with the snowy summit of Mount Olympus in full view, to Thessalonica, an important seaport and a large and thriving commercial city. There he found the Jews occupying a prominent position, and leavening the religious life of the community. Great indeed must have been their astonishment as they listened to his teaching. It was entirely new to them. What light he shed on their old prophets! What daring criticism of their venerable law! Luke has preserved for us a summary of his preaching: " That it behoved the Christ to suffer, and to rise again from the dead; and that this Jesus, whom I proclaim unto you, is the Christ" (Acts xvii. 3). In looking for an earthly Messiah who was to resuscitate the Jewish nation and restore its ancient glory, they had been indulging a hope to which their Scriptures gave no countenance. Paul showed them that the Messiah was to assume the form of a servant, was to be a man of sorrows, was to suffer a cruel death, but was to be raised from the dead and exalted to the highest position in the heavenly world. All that Paul assured them had actually happened in the person of Jesus of Nazareth whom he preached to them. On three successive Sabbaths he told in the synagogue the story of Jesus to an audience composed of Jews and Gentiles. A deep impression was produced, for although Jewish prejudice refused to be convinced, and offered a determined opposition to the Apostle, the Gentiles welcomed the glad tidings of salvation. Here were no silly stories of the infamous lives of the gods, here were no superstitious charms, here was no impressive ritual.

They were not asked to submit to such rites as prevented many of them from becoming Jews. Here was forgiveness of sins on the ground of what this Jesus had done, provided they were willing to accept Him as their Saviour. There was something so calm, so reasonable, so persuasive in the language and manner of the Apostle that many of them were convinced. They renounced their idolatry, they gave themselves up to the worship of the one living and true God, their faith accepted and rested on the work of Jesus, and their hopes were centred on His speedy return to this earth, to put an end to all the sufferings of His people and to receive them into His eternal kingdom.

It was indeed marvellous. "A full-grown Church established in the course of three or four weeks is doubtless a unique fact in missionary annals."[1] How was it to be explained? Only in one way: by the presence and power of the Holy Spirit. Paul was conscious of a heavenly afflatus when he preached to them. He felt carried away. He had no time to think of the form in which to present the truth. "The word of the Lord was a fire in his bones." "Our gospel came not unto you in word only, but also in power, and in the Holy Ghost, and in much assurance; even as ye know what manner of men we shewed ourselves toward you for your sakes" (I. i. 5). "Ye received the word of the message, even the word of God, ye accepted it not as the word of men, but, as it is

---

[1] Godet, *Studies in the Epistles*, p. 3.

in truth, the word of God, which also worketh in them that believe" (I. ii. 13). The careful reader of Paul's Epistles cannot fail to notice how he lays stress on the instrumentality of the word in the conversion of sinners. Not every one like himself was arrested and changed in a moment by the direct vision of the ascended Christ. In the majority of conversions God employs the reading and preaching of the Word to produce saving impressions on the sinner's heart.

Now it might be said that a change so suddenly brought about was apt to be superficial and transitory, and that the impressions produced by his preaching would fade away when Paul left Thessalonica. And indeed that was what the Apostle feared. He was exceedingly concerned for the steadfastness of his converts, especially as they were likely to be called to suffer for their adhesion to the new teaching. But when Timothy, whom he had left behind him to carry on the work, brought back to Corinth his glowing account of their steadfastness and progress in the Christian life, his mind was set free from all anxiety. The work in Thessalonica was tested by its fruit. And to this little Church Paul dictated, most probably to Timothy, the first of those letters which give us an insight into his large and loving heart. They are the outpouring of the man as well as of the inspired Apostle, very human in their tenderness and sometimes in their severity. The second letter followed not long after, and was intended to remove certain erroneous impressions produced by his first, which appears to have had an unsettling effect upon the lives of the Thessalonian converts.

Throughout these Epistles there is a singular gentleness and sweetness, and a marked absence of the severity and censure running through some of the others. The Church at Thessalonica was as yet free from the Judaising spirit. It had no doctrinal troubles. Its members were resting in the simple truths delivered to them by Paul, and they were living up to their faith. Their "work of faith and labour of love and patience of hope in our Lord Jesus Christ" were matters of continual thanksgiving (I. i. 3). They became an ensample of the Christian life to the Churches in Macedonia and Achaia (I. i. 7). Their faith was steadily growing, and so was their charity toward one another (II. i. 3).

Not the least remarkable feature of this Church, whose growth had been so surprising, was its missionary zeal. Conscious of the change produced in their own lives, they bore testimony both by word and example to the gospel of the Lord Jesus Christ, and soon the whole country heard the word of the Lord from them (I. i. 8–10).

What, then, was the gospel Paul preached at Thessalonica? Did it differ in any way from that which he preached in Galatia or in Ephesus or in Corinth, or which he more fully expounded in the Epistle to the Romans? The difference is only in form, not in matter. The gospel is presented in its simplest form in these Epistles, as Paul was accustomed to preach it in his missionary journeys.

We note the absence of controversial or argumentative terms. He sought to turn the hearts of men from their idols to God manifest in Jesus Christ. If he lays greater stress on the Christian's hope directed to the second coming of Jesus Christ, it is because of the interest that subject had in the mind of the Thessalonian Christians. We can trace, however, through these Epistles the conception of the gospel Paul had come to entertain, which formed the kernel of his preaching, and which is developed more fully in some of his other Epistles. "The most likely suggestion is that the Epistles to the Thessalonian Church show us the form in which Paul judged it fitting to present the gospel to nascent Christian communities, when he had in view merely their immediate religious needs and capacities, and had no occasion to guard them against errors and misconceptions."[1]

These Epistles reveal in its most elementary form the main point in Paul's conception of the gospel—salvation by the death of Christ. In his preaching at Thessalonica, as we have seen, Paul "alleged that the Christ must needs have suffered" (Acts xvii. 3), and in his First Epistle to this Church he repeats the same truth: "God appointed us not to wrath, but unto the obtaining of salvation through our Lord Jesus Christ, who died for us" (I. v. 9, 10). And the necessity for this death he states explicitly in another passage is "to deliver us from the wrath to come" (I. i. 10). This was the gospel revealed to Paul's own ex-

[1] Bruce, *Paul's Conception of Christianity*, p. 13.

perience as he prayed in the house of Judas in Damascus, and accepted by him in its simplicity. It appears in all his Epistles, but the kernel is here. He expounds his teaching more fully in the Epistle to the Romans. Writing to the Christians at Rome, he says: "The gospel is the power of God unto salvation to every one that believeth" (Rom. i. 16). And the necessity for this saving influence is to be found in the fact that the whole human race was under the wrath of God: "The wrath of God is revealed from heaven against all ungodliness and unrighteousness of men, who hold down the truth in unrighteousness" (Rom. i. 18). And it is so revealed because all men have sinned against Him, and have become guilty before Him. The wages of sin is death; and the Son of God became incarnate and died, the Just for the unjust, that He might reconcile them to God, and thus might make them partakers of the salvation provided for and offered to them; in other words, that He might deliver them from the wrath to come. For the wrath of God was something terribly real to the Apostle. He could not forget the awful fact of sin, especially as he saw its manifestation in the heathen cities of the ancient world. Against that the wrath of God was revealed. For God's wrath is just His hatred of sin, and it is seen in its most lurid light in the Cross of His Son, which furnishes at the same time the brightest manifestation of His love.

Thus in his first letter to the Churches Paul

makes salvation by the death of Christ, as he does in his later Epistles, the central point and leading idea of his teaching.[1]

Though the central point of Paul's gospel, the crucified Saviour did not exhaust it, and in this Epistle he dwells even more fully on the risen and ascended Christ. In Thessalonica, Paul preached mainly to Gentiles, to whom their religion offered no solace for the present and no hope for the future; for it is well known that the early converts were, for the most part, drawn from the lower classes and even from slaves. The gospel made little or no alteration in their earthly lot, rather had it brought upon them suffering and persecution. Now the gospel preached to them was a gospel of hope. The kingdom of the Lord Jesus Christ was not to be fully set up in their day. Its triumph, however, was sure. Jesus who died on Calvary was not dead. He was at the right hand of God. He was reigning over the spiritual world. He was accomplishing His purpose. He was subduing all things to Himself. And He was to come again to bring about the final defeat of His enemies, and to establish His kingdom throughout the whole earth.

[1] Godet, *Studies in the Epistle*, p. 28.

"The unanimous testimony of the Apostles is, that the sacrifice as the ground of our forgiveness centres itself in His death. . . . We have above all the distinct declaration of Paul—who has so emphasised and elaborated this thought that it is supposed by many to be his peculiar creation—that on this point he was but repeating and unfolding the faith of the first disciples and of the whole Church" (Dr. Forrest, *Christ of History and of Experience*, p. 228).

The keynote to these Epistles is the oft-recurring phrase: "the coming again of our Lord Jesus Christ." "Ye turned unto God from idols, to serve a living and true God, and to wait for His Son from heaven" (I. i. 10). "For what is our hope, or joy, or crown of glorying? Are not even ye, before our Lord Jesus Christ at His coming?" (I. ii. 19). "To the end that He might establish your hearts unblameable in holiness before our God and Father, at the coming of our Lord Jesus Christ with all His saints" (I. iii. 13). And in the familiar passage so often read over our dead, he dwells on the coming of Jesus Christ to gather together all His saints in the glory of His kingdom (I. iv. 13–18). And in this connection he more than forty times speaks of Jesus as our Lord Jesus Christ. These passages give us a glimpse into the condition and experience of the early Christians. We see the eyes of the Apostle and of his converts turned toward their risen Lord in eager expectancy of His reappearing. That indeed was the lively hope Jesus left to His Apostles when He was taken from them. The message of the angels on the day of His ascension was, "This Jesus, which was received up from you into heaven, shall so come in like manner as ye beheld Him going into heaven" (Acts i. 11). And it is evident that what the Apostles were looking for in these early days was not so much the coming of the Comforter, as the reappearing of Jesus Christ. It was only gradually that they became reconciled to the conviction that His coming was not to be at once, and that much required to be done by His

Church before the Saviour would return to the earth. At the same time Paul's frequent dwelling on this exalted theme had an unsettling effect on the minds of some of the Thessalonians. They had become indifferent to the common duties and affairs of this life, negligent and slothful in business, while others were distressed by the thought that some of their dear ones, who had died before the Lord's return, would not share in His triumph. To both these classes the Apostle has a word. He assures the one that the coming of the Lord was not to be so soon as they expected, though the actual time of His reappearance was His own secret, and would be most unexpected. Hence it should be the duty of all Christians to be faithfully attending to the ordinary affairs of life, and at the same time to be prepared to welcome their Master when He returned.

In a remarkable passage which has occasioned more controversy perhaps than any other portion of Scripture, Paul indicated that before the establishment of the Saviour's kingdom there would be a great apostasy under one whom he designates as "The Man of Sin" (II. ii. 3–10), who after a brief success would be at last subdued. Many have been the speculations as to the person so designated. Without attempting to answer the question, it is evident that the Apostle hints at the temporary triumph of the kingdom of darkness at some period immediately preceding the coming of Christ. But these dark days will pass away. The kingdom of God is destined to triumph over all the powers of wickedness opposed to its progress, and Jesus shall reign universal King, exalted above all principalities and powers, and every name that is named, not only in this world, but also in that which is to come.

To those who were grieving over the thought that their dead friends would not share in this triumph of the Saviour, he gives the assurance that both the living and the dead would participate in that glorious event. The appearance of Jesus in His glory was to be the signal for the opening of all the graves on earth and for the resurrection of His own people from the dead, to meet Him and accompany Him to His Father's house.

In Paul's conception of the gospel, as it finds expression in these Epistles, great importance is attached to its effect on the life of the believer. "God chose you from the beginning unto salvation in sanctification of the Spirit and belief of the truth" (II. ii. 13). "This is the will of God, even your sanctification" (I. iv. 3). "God called us not for uncleanness, but in sanctification" (I. iv. 7). The two things, salvation and sanctification, invariably go together in Paul's gospel. He knows of no salvation that does not include holiness of heart and life. He cannot imagine the moral condition of those who find in the gospel an encouragement to sin. Moral perfection, conformity to the image of God in Christ, is what the gospel aims at; and the earnest prayer of the Apostle for his Thessalonian converts finds expression in the sublime utterance, "And the God of peace Himself sanctify you wholly; and may your spirit and soul and body be preserved entire, without blame at the coming of our Lord Jesus Christ" (I. v. 23).

III

THE GOSPEL IN THE EPISTLES TO THE CORINTHIANS

THE religion of Jesus made a forward movement when it crossed the Ægean Sea and set foot on the shores of Greece. It thereby threw itself into conflict with the philosophy, the culture, and the civilisation of the West, which were closely allied with paganism. A bolder man might have shrunk from the attack, but Paul did not hesitate to meet the philosophers of Athens, who prided themselves on their learning and intellectual acumen, and to discuss with them the deepest truths of religion. His visit was not attended with much success, and with a feeling of disappointment he turned his back on the light-hearted people and the scoffing sages of Athens. Corinth was the next city in which he ventured to cross swords with the superstition and abominations of paganism. From its unrivalled situation, commanding the seas both to the east and west, and forming a link of communication between Northern and Southern Greece, Corinth had played a splendid part in the earlier history of

Greece; but about two hundred years before the Apostle set foot there, it had been captured by the Roman general Mummius, its treasures rifled, and the city itself reduced to a heap of ruins. Under the fostering care of Julius Cæsar it had been rebuilt and embellished, and at the time of the Apostle's visit was one of the most prosperous cities of the ancient world. Its inhabitants boasted of their ripe learning, their philosophic insight, and their ready wit. As a commercial city, Corinth had no rival. The trade of the East and West passed over its isthmus. Increasing wealth fostered increasing indulgence, and this in turn led to increasing immorality. To the widespread immorality, the religious worship most favoured there lent only too ready encouragement, so that the very name of the city became synonymous with the worst forms of vice. This city, the Apostle, when compelled to withdraw from Athens, entered one day, and having found a lodging, in which he wrought at his trade, with Aquila and Priscilla, like-minded friends, he proceeded on the Sabbath day to expound the doctrine of Christ in the synagogue. Meeting with little success among his own countrymen, Paul with fear and trembling addressed himself to the Greek population (I. ii. 3), and preached Christ to them: "For the Son of God, Jesus Christ, was preached among you by us" (II. i. 19).

It is apparent from the Epistles that not many of the wealthy merchants or of the haughty magnates were attracted by the views of a man who made his living by working at tent-making. His labours were confined for the most part to the poorer classes, and no doubt to the slaves who constituted a large part of the population, although we find mention of the chamberlain of the city as among his converts, and others who were in more prosperous circumstances (Rom. xvi. 23).

The refusal of Gallio, the Roman governor, to interfere with his liberty in prosecuting his mission was no doubt in the Apostle's favour, and the result of his work was a flourishing little Church, called by Godet "the most brilliant crown of his labours"; a Church in which he had the satisfaction of seeing the triumph of the gospel over the paganism which had held unchallenged sway in that city for centuries. He cared for that Church with all the tender solicitude of a nurse. He knew well the materials of which it was composed, the temptations by which it was beset, and he kept himself in close touch with its members by means of letters and messengers. These messengers had brought with them on one occasion a letter from the leaders of the Church, asking the Apostle's advice on certain questions affecting their relations with their heathen neighbours, but keeping silent on some disorders that had crept into the Church. These disorders had been brought under his notice by some of his friends at Corinth; and it was with a view to answer these questions and to correct these irregularities that the Apostle penned his letters, in which he shows most admirably the adaptation of the gospel of Christ to all conditions of life, whether among the Jews or the Greeks, whether in the East or in the West. The doctrinal element is not so prominent as the practical. There are few direct references to Christ and His work, no lengthened arguments to defend his gospel, if we except the great passage bearing on the doctrine of the Resurrection; but he makes it very clear that the gospel he preached was the simple gospel of Jesus Christ, what he calls the "simplicity that is towards Christ," the same gospel as he preached in Galatia and in Thessalonica. Here it is essentially a practical gospel he sets before the Corinthians, resting on the great facts of Christ's life and teaching, presented not in the strict logical form in which it appears in the Epistle to the Romans, but in a more natural way, as it might best meet the questions he was seeking to answer.

In what form, then, had Paul preached the gospel to the men of Corinth? They, too, like the Athenians, boasted of their wisdom. It was a common saying that no one could walk the streets of Corinth without encountering a sage. Did he then seek to recommend his gospel in the polished phrases of a fine rhetoric? Did he present it in a manner likely to tickle the ears and intellects of his learned hearers? By no means. He had had enough of this. He had spoken in that fashion to the philosophers of Athens. To them he had addressed a skilfully-framed speech, in which he had shown his acquaintance with their literature and learning. Perhaps on that occasion he had trusted too much to his own powers of speech, and the result certainly was not satisfactory. He made little impression on his hearers. In Corinth he adopted another method. He told his story simply, and let it produce its own effect. He did not trust to the words of his own wisdom, but to the inherent power of the truth, and to the accompanying influence of the Spirit of God. Well he knew that his own countrymen would stumble at his story, and that the Greeks would ridicule it. For it was the story of the Cross; it was Jesus Christ and Him crucified that he made the leading subject of his preaching. "And I, brethren, when I came unto you, came not with excellency of speech or of wisdom, proclaiming to you the mystery of God. For I determined to know nothing among you, save Jesus Christ, and Him crucified" (I. ii. 1, 2). And he defines his gospel more fully and explains the preaching of the Cross. "Now I make known unto you the gospel which I preached unto you. . . . For I delivered unto you first of all that which also I received, how that Christ died for our sins according to the Scriptures; and that He was buried; and that He hath been raised on the third day according to the Scriptures; and that He appeared to Cephas; then to the twelve" (I. xv. 1–5). That gospel, which to many of them was foolishness, had proved itself the power of God to salvation to not a few who had been delivered thereby from the pollution of heathenism and had been washed, sanctified, and justified in the name of the Lord Jesus Christ.

The gospel Paul preached at Corinth was a gospel of reconciliation. Men were enemies of

God, alienated in their minds by wicked works, and he had come to Corinth as an ambassador from God Himself with a message of reconciliation, to beseech them in Christ's stead to give up their sinful ways and to be reconciled to God, who had given proof of the earnestness of His desire for their reconciliation by making "Jesus Christ, who knew no sin, to be sin on our behalf, that we might become the righteousness of God in Him" (II. v. 20, 21). His gospel to the Corinthians was therefore a gospel of salvation from sin by the death of Jesus; the same gospel preached by Peter and John and the other Apostles. Nothing could be simpler or more devoid of the appearance of human wisdom. If it did not suit the men of culture in Corinth, it was eagerly embraced by many of the poor and base and despised, who rejoiced at the simplicity and purity that is toward Christ, because it assured them of present deliverance from sin and of a future happiness altogether undreamed of in their present condition.

It was necessary, too, to remind the members of the Church at Corinth, who had been gathered in from the pollution of heathenism, as he had reminded the Galatians, that the salvation of the gospel was deliverance from a sinful life as well as from the guilt of sin. Paul's messengers had informed him that certain forms of sin were being winked at by the Corinthian Christians, and so he had to remind them of the sacredness of the body, which shared in the redemption of Jesus Christ, and which ought therefore to be as carefully guarded as the soul: "Know ye not that your body is a temple of the Holy Ghost which is in you, which ye have from God?" (I. vi. 19). Redeemed by Jesus Christ they no longer belonged to themselves, and were bound to place themselves at the disposal of their Master, to do always those things which were well-pleasing to Him. "Ye are not your own; for ye were bought with a price: glorify God therefore in your body" (I. vi. 20). And, as if that were not enough, he appeals to the great love of Christ as the all-constraining motive to a life of self-denial and holiness amid their sinful surroundings: "For the love of Christ constraineth us; because we thus judge, that one died for all, therefore all died; and He died for all, that they which live should no longer live unto themselves, but unto Him who for their sakes died and rose again" (II. v. 14, 15).

Again, he finds in his simple gospel the means of healing the unhappy divisions that had taken place among the members of the Church at Corinth. In his own absence from the city he had despatched Apollos thither, who had laboured with great earnestness and success. He was "a learned man and mighty in the Scriptures," and, from his early training at Alexandria, may have been led to present the gospel in a manner more acceptable to lovers of wisdom like the Corinthians. Whatever may have been the cause of it—and we cannot for a moment suppose that Apollos lent himself to the movement—a party had been formed in Corinth which exalted the preaching of Apollos above that of Paul, and called itself by his name. Some of the Jewish converts had formed another party which attached more importance to the Mosaic law than Paul had done, and supported their action by the authority of Cephas, whose name they took; while others harped back to the sayings of Jesus Himself, and insisting on the discrepancy between the teaching of Jesus and that of the Apostle, called themselves by the name of Christ. What was Paul to do? The simplicity of the gospel was in danger of being corrupted by the numerous parties, all grounding their teaching on the gospel. He dealt with it in his own noble and unselfish spirit. In the erection of a house more importance is attached to the foundation on which it rests and the material of which it is built than to the person of the builder. So it did not matter so much who had been used by God to lead them to the knowledge of the truth. The question for them to consider was, Were they building on the right foundation? Were they resting on Jesus Christ and Him crucified? For Christian faith does not rest on Paul or Apollos or Cephas, but on Jesus Christ: "Other foundation can no man lay than that which is laid, which is Jesus Christ" (I. iii. 11).

In connection with another evil, Paul was led to give to the Corinthians that simple and comprehensive account of the Lord's Supper which is now the recognised rule for its observance in Protestant Churches, and contains the very essence of his gospel. Some of the Corinthians were in the habit of attending idolatrous feasts given by their heathen friends, and thus seemed to countenance idolatry. Others by carrying many of their old customs into their own feasts, had shamefully abused the Lord's Supper. They turned it into an ordinary meal, at which they ate and drank immoderately. Paul therefore felt it necessary to separate the ordinance of the Supper altogether from a house meal and to make it distinctly a Church institution; but there is not a word about offering up a sacrifice to God. There is not a word about the presence of a priest. There is not a word about the cup being confined to the priest. It is a commemorative ordinance, in which the believer remembers the death of Jesus. "This is My body, which is for you: this do in remembrance of Me. This cup is the new covenant in My blood: this do, as often as ye drink it, in remembrance of Me. For as often as ye eat this bread, and drink the cup, ye proclaim the Lord's death till He come" (I. xi. 24-26).

Even in enforcing the duty of liberally supporting the poorer members of the Church, the Apostle finds a motive in the gospel he preached: "Ye know the grace of our Lord Jesus Christ, that, though He was rich, yet for your sakes He became poor, that ye through His poverty might become rich" (II. viii. 9). The humiliation of Christ was for the exaltation and enrichment of His people.

No part of Paul's teaching proved such a stumbling-block to the Greek mind as his doctrine of the resurrection of the body. The Greeks believed in the immortality of the soul, and often discussed the question; but the resurrection of the body seemed to them incredible. It is true they paid great attention to the body, to its physical training and development, but they had never dreamed of its being raised from the tomb. Why, then, did Paul lay such stress upon the doctrine of the resurrection? Because it was implied in the great historical fact of which he and the other Apostles were witnesses—the resurrection of Jesus Christ from the dead. If Jesus had not risen again from the dead, then the whole gospel which Paul preached was a delusion. The gospel of Jesus Christ and Him crucified was valueless unless alongside of it he could present the gospel of Jesus Christ raised from the dead and exalted to the right hand of God in the heavenly places. Of this glorious fact Paul had no doubt, and he briefly summarises the evidence for it: "He was crucified through weakness, yet He liveth by the power of God" (II. xiii. 4). And on that fact he built, to use the words of Godet, "the whole glorious edifice of Christian hope, the resurrection of believers on the coming again of Jesus Christ, the ultimate destruction of death by the universal resurrection, after Christ shall have overthrown, in His millenarian reign, all His enemies; and then the final act, when, the mediatorial reign being ended, Christ shall deliver up the kingdom to His Father, that God may be all in all to the sanctified believers."[1] Still there remained the almost insuperable objection to the resurrection of the material or natural body. Paul met this by the statement that as the body of

[1] Godet, *Studies in the Epistles*, p. 93.

the risen Saviour was a spiritual body, so shall the resurrection body be. The body of the flesh dissolved in the grave shall not be raised again, but a spiritual body into which the essence of the old has entered, and which has preserved its identity. The change is not so impossible as it seems. It has its analogy in the operation of nature. When we sow a grain of wheat, the actual seed dies; it passes through the stage of corruption, but out of it, composed of the same elements, grows the new stalk of wheat, the new body in which the old seed has clothed itself. To this glorious event, as he tells us in another Epistle, the whole renewed creation is looking forward. It sees its aspirations and longings blighted by death. The path of light appears to end in the darkness, and the believer wonders what is to be the end of all things. Into that darkness Jesus has shed a great light. There is an exit as well as an entrance to the grave. If the one leads into darkness, the other leads into the everlasting light of God's countenance. "Thanks be to God, which giveth us the victory through our Lord Jesus Christ" (I. xv. 57). Strong in this hope, the blossom and fruit of the gospel he preached, the Apostle closed his First Epistle with the words: "Our Lord cometh. The grace of the Lord Jesus Christ be with you. My love be with you all in Christ Jesus" (I. xvi. 23, 24).

IV

THE GOSPEL IN THE EPISTLE TO THE GALATIANS

IN Acts xvi. 6 and xviii. 23 mention is made of two visits paid by Paul to the country or region of Galatia; and until very recently it was generally understood that by that name was designated the northern province, the population of which was for the most part Celtic. It seemed on the face of it somewhat strange that he should turn aside from a work which had been attended with wonderful success to a people of a different race altogether, and to a region where he was less likely to meet with his own countrymen, in whose synagogues he generally commenced his mission. It was found difficult, too, to account for the contents of the Epistle on the supposition that it was addressed to a Church in the northern province. Largely owing to the investigations of Professor Ramsay it is now known that the name of the Roman province of Galatia embraced, in addition to the northern province, the countries of Phrygia,

Lycaonia, and Pisidia, and included therefore the Churches of Antioch in Pisidia, Iconium, Lystra, and Derbe — Churches founded by Paul and Barnabas, in whose welfare he continued to take the deepest interest. This is now the generally received view with regard to the destination of the Epistle, and it supplies a felt want in the life-history of the Apostle. Every reader of the Acts of the Apostles knows of the remarkable success attending the first missionary journey of Paul and Barnabas to Asia Minor, and of the deep interest he continued to take in the Churches founded during that journey. He returned again and again to Antioch in Pisidia, to Iconium, and to Derbe and Lystra. Some of his best workers were drawn from these Churches, and in them the Jewish element was very prominent. On the North Galatian theory it seemed almost unaccountable that the Apostle should have addressed no communication to Churches so dear to his own heart. The difficulty, however, disappears if we accept the view that this letter was written to these Churches. The origin and contents of the Epistle become intelligible, read in this light; for the historian in the Acts has not a word to say about the people of the northern province. He throws no side-light on the Epistle if it was sent to that district. He furnishes no key to its deeply interesting teaching. He has, however, made us familiar with Paul's visits to Antioch, Iconium, Derbe, and Lystra, and with the fierce controversies raging at the time this Epistle was penned, and thus gives us a key to unlock the meaning of this important letter.

It is evident from the Epistle (Gal. iv. 13–15) that the Galatians had received the Apostle on his first visit with open arms, and had eagerly accepted the gospel he preached to them: "Ye received me as an angel of God, even as Christ Jesus." "I bear you witness, that, if possible, ye would have plucked out your eyes and given them to me." This is quite in keeping with the historian's account of Paul's visit to Antioch, etc. The Gentiles were filled with joy when they learned that Paul had acceded to their request to preach to them the same gospel he had hitherto proclaimed in the synagogue of his own countrymen, and they gave a hearty welcome to his message: "And when the Gentiles heard this, they were glad, and glorified the word of God" (Acts xiii. 48). In Derbe and Lystra the two Apostles were received as gods by the simple-hearted people, who, however, with the proverbial fickleness of an Eastern crowd, afterwards stoned Paul.

In his second missionary journey Paul bore to these Churches the decree of the Jerusalem Church as to the conditions on which the Gentiles were to be received into the Church. When he left them he was immediately succeeded by certain Judaising teachers, who deliberately set themselves to undo his work in these Churches. To these men he refers in the Epistle as "preaching another gospel" (i. 8, 9). "False brethren privily brought in, who came in privily to spy out our liberty which we have in Christ Jesus" (ii. 4). These brethren went about calling in question the apostolic authority of Paul, and representing him as differing in his teaching from the other Apostles. They assured the Galatians that while Paul did not require them to accept the law of Moses in order to join the Christian Church, he insisted on this in the case of all whom he deemed worthy of the highest teaching and the highest life. Paul, according to them, was a trimmer and a time-server, suiting his gospel to the circumstances of the people among whom he laboured, insisting on the observance of the Jewish law when the Jews were in the majority, and not requiring this when the Gentiles were the more numerous. These false teachers, ignoring the decree of the Council of Jerusalem, insisted on the Gentile Christians submitting to the Mosaic law and ritual; and as it is quite possible that, on their conversion, they may have felt the want of their old heathen ritual and ceremonies, there may have been for some of them a considerable attraction in the return to the ceremonial of the Jewish worship.

It was with considerable sorrow and anxiety that Paul heard of the success of these false brethren among his converts in the Galatian Churches. It cut him to the heart that the converts over whom he had rejoiced, who had showed him such affection, and who had given such good promise in the Christian life, had forgotten all his teaching, and had been led away by the zealous advocates of the old religion; and so he took up his pen, and sent to them this letter to counteract the influence of these false brethren privily brought in. His deep emotion shows itself through the whole letter; his heart throbs in his words. There is a holy indignation burning in some of his sentences, and a tone of scathing rebuke in others. He would have these false brethren and evil-disposed persons, who had disturbed their faith, cut off; and pronounces a solemn curse on those who dared to preach a gospel other than that which he had delivered to them.

This letter, then, is a defence, an apology, a rebuke, and an earnest exhortation. It is a defence of the gospel as Paul understood it, and which he earnestly entreated the Galatians to hold fast as the charter of their liberty. Professor Godet calls it "the manifesto of the spiritual enfranchisement won by Christ for all believers."

Some of these false brethren privily brought in had insinuated that as the latest Apostle, one born out of due time, and one who in all probability owed his knowledge of Christ and His gospel to the other Apostles, his teaching was not possessed of the same authority as that of the first disciples of Jesus Christ. If that were true, no one knew better than he how it would strike at the root of all his teaching, and afford good ground for the distinction that might be made between his gospel and that proclaimed by Jesus and His immediate followers. He therefore in the very beginning of his letter boldly and unhesitatingly claimed for his teaching the same authority claimed by the other Apostles. It is true he had grown up a bigoted opponent of Jesus of Nazareth. But it was Jesus Himself who had appeared to him in person, who had convinced him of His risen and glorified life, and had revealed to him the message he was to deliver to his fellow-men: "I certify you, brethren, that the gospel which was preached of me is not after man. For I neither received it of man, neither was I taught it, but by the revelation of Jesus Christ" (i. 11, 12).

If he owed anything to any man it must have been to the martyred Stephen, to whose defence he had listened, whose dying testimony to the glorified Son of Man was indelibly stamped on his mind. He disclaimed, however, the teaching of any man. The truth dawned upon him gradually, as in the solitudes of Arabia he studied the Scriptures under the guidance of the Holy Spirit. And it is interesting to note how Paul, searching the Scriptures for himself, came to take the same view of Jesus as the disciples who had been taught by the Master.

What, then, was the gospel Paul had proclaimed to the Galatian Churches, and which he presents in this Epistle? In the Acts of the Apostles we find it stated thus in the synagogue of Antioch in Pisidia: "Be it known unto you therefore, brethren, that through this man is proclaimed unto you remission of sins" (Acts xiii. 38). "I have set thee for a light of the Gentiles, that thou shouldest be for salvation unto the uttermost part of the earth" (xiii. 47). And in this letter he tells the Galatians in his opening words that "our Lord Jesus Christ gave Himself for our sins, that He might deliver us out of this present evil world, according to the will of our God and Father" (i. 4); and he closes with the confident assertion, "Far be it from me to glory, save in the Cross of our Lord Jesus Christ" (vi. 14). These two statements form the keynote of the whole Epistle. The gospel which he preached was the gospel of redemption, of deliverance, of freedom. In the Epistle to the Romans, as we shall see, it was the gospel of a complete atonement that Paul set before the converts in that city. In the Epistles to the Corinthians it was the gospel of reconciliation, by which the sinner was at once restored to the favour of God, and the gospel ministry was defined as a ministry of reconciliation. In this Epistle Paul's aim was to show the Galatians that the gospel was a scheme of redemption or deliverance. Its object was to deliver men from the bondage of guilt in which the convinced sinner is held. "Howbeit the Scripture hath shut up all things under sin, that the promise by faith in Jesus Christ might be given to them that believe" (iii. 22). It was, as Godet calls it, "the Act of Emancipation of the slaves of the law in all ages." If indeed it was impossible to obtain acceptance with God through the deeds of the law, because "cursed was every one which continueth not in all things that are written in the book of the law, to do them" (iii. 10), Paul could assure the sinner that "Christ redeemed us from the curse of the law, having become a curse for us" (iii. 13). The old form of rites and ceremonies is no longer binding, for it is not obedience to these that is to secure his acceptance with God, but faith in Jesus, who has borne the penalty of the broken law, and has brought him into the glorious liberty of the new dispensation. Under the gospel we are not slaves, but children. We have received the child's heart, we breathe the spirit of children, and our service of God is now a service of love, in which we are delivered from the galling bondage of the law, meant for slaves and for children who were not yet of age. For this is the great privilege the gospel has brought us. It restores us again to our position as the children of God. "When the fulness of the time came, God sent forth His Son, born of a woman, born under the law, that He might redeem them which were under the law." The law had its own use. In intensifying the consciousness of sin it deepened the conviction of the impossibility of righteousness by the deeds of the law, and it thus, like the slave who in Greek towns led his master's child to school, brought the convinced sinner to Christ. But now that Christ has received him, he needs this leader no longer.

No wonder the Apostle is so fond of dwelling on this aspect of the gospel, and entreats his converts never to dream of any return to that old bondage. In their heathen state they had been under the bondage of degrading superstitions, and now they were being invited by these false teachers, after they had tasted the liberty of the gospel, to place themselves again under the grievous yoke of ceremony. "Stand fast therefore," he implores them, "and be not entangled again in a yoke of bondage" (v. 1).

Such a presentation of the gospel is of invaluable service to the Church in all ages; for it is ever exposed to this same danger of accepting the yoke of ceremony for the yoke of Christ. It is so much easier for some men to trust to ceremonies and ordinances diligently observed than to the Saviour Himself, and to the purifying of the heart by faith. Now in thus insisting on the gospel of liberty, Paul was re-echoing the teaching of his Master. Almost in the same terms had Jesus asserted the freedom of the gospel He had come to proclaim. His enemies would have tied Him down to the restrictions with which they had surrounded the law, but He reminded them that the truth makes men free. He reminded them of the glorious liberty He had come to proclaim: "If the Son shall make you free, ye shall be free indeed" (John viii. 36). "Take My yoke upon you, and learn of Me. . . . For My yoke is easy, and My burden is light" (Matt. xi. 30).

Further, the gospel was a gospel of freedom from sin. It aimed at deliverance from a sinful life as well as from the curse of the law. This, too, was an essential element of the gospel as Paul understood it. He repudiated the slanderous imputation that he was encouraging a sinful life by preaching this gospel of liberty. Nothing could be further from his intention, nothing further from the truth. Replying to the question, " Is Christ a minister of sin ? " (ii. 17), he says: " I through the law died unto the law, that I might live unto God " (ii. 18). And in one of his sublimest utterances he speaks of himself as having been nailed with Jesus to the Cross, and consequently as having paid with Him the penalty of sin ; but he is conscious now of a new life—a life that is not his own, a life proceeding from the indwelling of Christ in him, which therefore resembles His life as far as it is possible for the life of any sinful man to resemble that of the incarnate Saviour. " I have been crucified with Christ ; yet I live ; and yet no longer I, but Christ liveth in me : and that life which I now live in the flesh I live in faith, the faith which is in the Son of God, who loved me, and gave Himself up for me " (ii. 20). The liberty of the gospel is not licence : " Use not your freedom for an occasion to the flesh " (v. 13). If any professing Christian continue to live a sinful life, and to do the works of the flesh, he shows that far from having entered into the freedom of the gospel, he is still in bondage to the flesh. Whereas if a man be really led by the Spirit of God, if he live the life of the Spirit, and bring forth in his daily life the fruits of the Spirit, he gives the best possible evidence that he is in the enjoyment of the glorious liberty of the children of God.

This was the gospel committed to him by Jesus

Christ which Paul proclaimed in season and out of season. He was accused of altering the gospel to suit the peoples among whom he laboured, of attaching no importance, in his teaching, to the ordinance of circumcision, and yet of imposing it upon Timothy. What he virtually says is in illustration of this freedom of the gospel. "Timothy's mother was a Jewess. I attach no importance to the rite, but as, by submitting to it, he would have greater influence in labouring among Jews, I was quite willing that he should be circumcised; but as many of you, the Galatians, have never been under that yoke, I protest against your now being subjected to it." Far from pleasing men in his office, Paul affirmed that he was the devoted servant of Jesus Christ. In the Epistles to the Corinthians he magnified his sufferings for Jesus' sake. He boasted of his infirmities, reproaches, necessities, persecutions, and distresses for Jesus' sake. Here he simply speaks of himself as the slave of Jesus Christ, whose marks he bore in his body, the marks of suffering received in his visit to Galatia, which he would carry with him to the grave. The false teachers who were trying to enslave the Galatians had no other object than to glorify themselves. They hoped to report their success in opposing the gospel Paul preached. But Paul's ambition was higher. He lost sight of self in his Master, whom he had openly set forth crucified: "Far be it from me to glory, save in the Cross of our Lord Jesus Christ" (vi. 14). This is the great end of all gospel preaching—to hold up to men Jesus Christ, who by His death on the Cross has for ever taken away their sin. This was the gospel of Paul—a gospel which requires not only reliance on Christ, but allegiance to Christ; for the Cross is not only a banner around which the followers of Jesus may rally; it is not only a name to inspire confidence; it is a power making for holiness; it is that by which the world is crucified to us, and we unto the world.

V

THE GOSPEL IN THE EPISTLE TO THE ROMANS

AT the time of the birth of Jesus Christ, he would have been viewed as an impracticable dreamer who dared to assert in the imperial city that the occupant of the manger in Bethlehem would one day wield the sceptre of universal dominion. Yet events as unlikely had occurred in the history of Rome. The son of a slave had risen to exercise supreme authority over the Roman people. The Child born in Bethlehem was not indeed to occupy any earthly throne, but the truth He proclaimed was to receive something like universal recognition, and His life and work were to have a world-wide influence. In the course of His earthly life Jesus Himself came in contact with the powers of Rome. His noble character, His self-conscious authority, the obedience He demanded and received, made a deep impression on the centurion of Capernaum. An impression equally deep though less permanent was made on Pilate, the Roman governor, when Jesus was brought as a prisoner to his tribunal, and before him Jesus had the opportunity of pressing His claims and proclaiming the true nature of His mission. At the same time it is not likely that anything was heard in Rome of such an everyday event as the crucifixion of a poor Jew at Jerusalem. Pilate would no doubt report the event, but the attention of the authorities would not be otherwise called to it. A seditious movement had been nipped in the bud, its leader had been crucified, and nothing more was likely to be heard of him or of his cause. But it was not dead, and on that memorable day when the power of the risen Saviour was manifested by the gift of the Holy Spirit, amongst those who listened to the first gospel sermon preached by Peter were strangers of Rome, who carried back the story of the Cross, the story of the man Jesus, who lived a blameless life, who wrought such wonderful works, who had been put to a shameful death, but who was now alive again performing by His followers mighty works, and declared by them to be able to save the worst sinner from his sins. The story spread, chiefly we may be sure among the industrial and poorer classes, but also among the soldiers. Little groups of Christians gathered in private houses (xvi. 4, 14, 16), where they worshipped Christ. Defective as their knowledge of the gospel was in the absence of any qualified teacher, they were distinguished for the strength of their faith, the warmth of their love, and their devotion to Jesus Christ (i. 8). There is nothing to support the catholic tradition that Rome owed its possession of the gospel to the preaching of the Apostle Peter; and it is certain that if he ever visited the imperial city it was near the close of his life. Paul, however, had heard of the progress of the gospel in Rome, and as one commissioned to go far hence to the Gentiles, had early formed the design of preaching the gospel in the capital of the world (Acts xix. 21; Rom. i. 10, 13, 15). The world was ruled from Rome. The trend of thought at Rome influenced the thought of the world. The provinces accepted the fashions prevalent at Rome, and were quite prepared to honour in their temples the latest deity who had found favour at Rome. If therefore the gospel could obtain a hold at Rome, if it could influence the national mind or even excite the popular curiosity, if it should come to leaven the life of the community, who could say what a blessed influence it might have on the whole empire. Rome therefore became the goal of his ambition, but he had been prevented from reaching it; and so when he had finished his third great missionary journey and was contemplating his last visit to Jerusalem, he resolved to write a letter to these humble Christians at Rome, intimating his intended visit, and setting before them in the clearest possible terms the great truths of that gospel he longed to communicate by word of mouth.

To form an estimate of this wonderful Epistle, called by Coleridge "the most profound writing extant," we must have some idea of the Church to which he was writing, and his purpose in so writing. Was it, as Godet puts it, "in order to give in a written form to a body of Christians with whom he had not come into personal contact, the instruction which he had given *vivâ voce* to the Churches in Ephesus, Thessalonica, and Corinth"? Or was it, as Dr. Bruce contends, to counteract the Judaising teachers who had found their way to Rome and were unsettling the minds of the little Christian community? The latter is the more likely view, and it is not inconsistent with his purpose that in carrying it out the Apostle had a wider design and aimed at giving to this Church a full and reasonable exposition of the gospel as the power of God to salvation. He was writing for a wider circle than the few Christians then in Rome. He knew the time was coming when even the pagan community might read and study it. He knew the time was coming when the Church, emerging from its long struggle with paganism, would need such an exposition of the central truths of the gospel. And if the time should ever come, as Paul confidently anticipated, when Rome should embrace the doctrines of the Crucified, the gospel would exercise a commanding influence on the Christian Church everywhere; and so he was anxious to lay a broad and sure foundation of truth on which to build the Church of Christ at Rome.

What adds special value to the Epistle is that in it we have a compendium of the gospel and of the teaching of Christ, formed by those who lived nearest to the time of Christ, and by a man who always maintained that he had received his gospel from Jesus Christ. It may present views of the gospel not to be found in the teaching of Jesus, but which are complementary and in many cases the logical outcome of that teaching. In fact it may be said that the elements of the Pauline theology as expressed in the Epistle to the Romans may all be found in the third chapter of the Gospel of John. And it is refreshing to find how clear and explicit this Epistle is upon those great themes which it is customary to include in gospel preaching—ruin by the Fall, redemption by the work of Jesus Christ, and regeneration by the Divine Spirit. Of those truths Paul tells us he was not ashamed, for in his experience they had proved the power of God to salvation to every one who believed.

The keynote to the whole Epistle may be found in i. 16, 17: " I am not ashamed of the gospel: for it is the power of God to salvation to every one that believeth; to the Jew first, and also to the Greek. For therein is revealed a righteousness of God by faith unto faith : as it is written, But the righteous shall live by faith." The gospel is thus with Paul a revelation of God's righteousness to man for his salvation, received and appropriated by faith alone. In what sense it reveals the righteousness of God is a disputed question, to which various answers have been given; some affirming that the redeeming work of Christ revealed the righteousness of God, who pledged Himself to save us, not as though the inherent abstract righteousness of God could necessitate His intervention

for the salvation of men, but because God from the
first made Himself known to man as a Saviour;[1]
others holding "God's righteousness, in Paul's
sense, does not appear to signify God's personal
righteousness, or our personal righteousness conceived of as well-pleasing to God, but a righteousness
which God gives to those who believe in Jesus."[2]
In both senses Jesus actually did in His death
reveal the righteousness of God. God was seen to
be righteous, and the believing sinner is declared
righteous because of the death of Christ on the
Cross. This revelation of God's righteousness was
rendered necessary by condemnation resting upon
the whole human race, upon the Gentile world
of which the Apostle gives the most appalling
description, and upon the Jewish nation which,
with all its advantages, had shamefully abused its
privileges and violated in spirit the law of God.
Everywhere he saw a world lying in wickedness, on
which the divine verdict had long since been pronounced: "There is none righteous, no, not one;
there is none that understandeth, there is none
that seeketh after God; they have all turned
aside, they are together become unprofitable; there
is none that doeth good, not so much as one" (iii.
11–13). Was this condition of the race hopeless,
and was its only outlook the revelation of the
wrath of God? Salvation was not to be found in
obedience to the divine law, for perfect obedience
in the future could never atone for the sins of the

---

[1] Principal Robertson, *Expositor*, Fifth Series, ix. p. 197.
[2] Bruce, *Paul's Conception of Christianity*, p. 114.

past. "By the works of the law shall no flesh be justified in His sight" (iii. 20). But what man could never do God has done. "For God hath shut up all unto disobedience, that He might have mercy on all" (xi. 32). "But now," says the Apostle, "apart from the law a righteousness of God hath been manifested, being witnessed by the law and the prophets; even the righteousness of God through faith in Jesus Christ unto all them that believe; for there is no distinction; for all have sinned, and come short of the glory of God: being justified freely by His grace through the redemption that is in Christ Jesus: whom God set forth to be a propitiation, through faith, by His blood, to shew His righteousness, because of the passing over of the sins done aforetime, in the forbearance of God; for the shewing, I say, of His righteousness at this present season: that He might Himself be just, and the justifier of him that hath faith in Jesus" (iii. 21–26).

This is Paul's gospel. In these few but comprehensive words we have the whole of his conception of the salvation that is by Jesus Christ. It is a manifestation of the righteousness of God. His law had pronounced sentence of condemnation on the transgressor. Were He merely to extend a free pardon to all transgressors He might be accused of injustice. But now that Jesus Christ has in His life made a full manifestation of the righteousness of God, by perfect obedience to His holy law, and now that, as the representative of a fallen race, Jesus has by His blood most fully atoned for the sin of man, God is only manifesting His righteousness when He extends pardon to those who by faith accept Jesus as their Saviour and surrender themselves to Him. It is a gospel of propitiation (Rom. iii. 24–26). "Whether we take ἱλαστήριον as a noun (a propitiatory victim) or as a neuter adjective, signifying a means of propitiation, the sense remains the same. The old interpretation which regarded it, not as the sin-offering, but (following the Septuagint usage) as the mercy-seat, is now generally given up as alien to Paul's method of thought."[1] Salvation is through the propitiatory sacrifice of Jesus Christ who gave Himself to death for man's redemption. The righteousness and the mercy of God meet and blend in the Cross. There the wrath of God is revealed, and there Jesus as the propitiation reveals His infinite love: "For God commendeth His own love toward us, in that, while we were yet sinners, Christ died for us" (v. 8). And if it be asked how could the righteousness of one pass over to all? Paul was ready with his reply. The transgression of one has passed unto all and all are under condemnation. Is there anything more mysterious in the righteousness of one passing unto all and the acquittal or, to use Paul's phrase, the justification of all, that accompanies that?

Another cardinal truth in Paul's gospel is the

[1] Dr. Forrest, *Christ of History and of Experience*, note p. 222. Bruce, *St. Paul's Conception of Christianity*, p. 168. "But even on this rendering the fundamental idea which underlies the word must be that of propitiation" (*International Crit. Comm. on Romans*, p. 91).

justification of the sinner by faith. On this he lays great stress. God is the "justifier of him that hath faith in Christ" (iii. 26). "Being justified by faith." Faith is thus the only condition of salvation possible for sinners. "It is," says Dr. Bruce, "faith in Christ as the embodiment of divine grace. It is further indicated that that in Christ Jesus, on which the eye of faith is chiefly fixed, is the redemption achieved by His death, wherein the grace of God to the sinful manifests itself. According to this passage, therefore, the faith that justifies is not simply faith in God, or faith in God's grace, or faith in the truth that Jesus is the Christ, but faith in Jesus as one who gave Himself to death for man's redemption, and so became the channel through which God's grace flows to sinners."[1] It is this faith that restores the sinner to the standing of a righteous man before God, to whom there is now no condemnation, and who has entered into peace with God through Jesus Christ.

Now, no doubt, the terms in which the Apostle thus states his gospel are his own, but the truths contained in it are found in the teaching of Christ. He, too, reminded men of the wrath of God revealed against all unrighteousness; He, too, shut up all men under sin; He, too, spoke of Himself as giving His life a ransom for many; He, too, declared that He was to be lifted up for the redemption of sinners, and the benefits of His salvation were to be enjoyed by those alone who believed in Him. In the one case Jesus simply

[1] Bruce, *Paul's Conception of Christianity*, p. 152.

stated the facts; Paul in his gospel reasons them out and shuts up the sinner, whether Jew or Gentile, to faith in the atoning death of Jesus as the only means of salvation. For this salvation is commensurate with the need of the race; all have sinned and are under condemnation; but this salvation avails for all, and is freely offered to all, for the Roman in his deep moral degradation as well as for the Jew in covenant relationship with the God of his fathers.

Justification—the placing of the sinner in a right relation with God—is not, however, the only blessing which he receives through faith in Jesus Christ. It is no doubt all-important that he realise this as the ground of his peace and joy and hope. By his faith he becomes also united to Christ, and a partaker of the life and spirit of Christ. The sinner by faith has died with Christ to sin. By faith, too, he has risen with Him to a new life, and feels constrained by his love to live for Him and to do that which is pleasing in His sight. He continues, indeed, to have within him remains of indwelling sin, which are a constant pain to him; but he is assured of his final triumph through that Saviour who died for him, and who ever lives to befriend and help him.

And this faith introduces the believer to that fuller blessedness and grace into which he has access through Jesus Christ. He passes from the bondage of sin into the full liberty of the children of God. He receives the name, the spirit, and the privileges of a child of God, the heir of all his Father's blessedness. He has entered into a union with Christ closer than that which exists in any other relation. No power in earth or heaven can ever separate him from the love of God in Christ. He fights a winning battle, for by his side is the Captain of his salvation, who makes him more than conqueror, while his soul is filled with peace and joy and hope—the sweetest blessings man can enjoy on earth.

Such is a sketch of the gospel Paul preached, and which he so carefully expounds to the Roman Christians. No wonder he was eager to preach it at Rome also. What visions he may have had of success in that city! What dreams of the future awaiting the little Church in the capital! His arrest in Jerusalem altered all his plans, and took from him his freedom. Galling as his imprisonment must have been, it was graciously tempered. A message of hope was sent to him that he was to be a witness for Christ at Rome. He entered the city as a prisoner, and was eagerly welcomed by the Christian community. They were not ashamed of his chains. They showed him every kindness. Possibly owing to the good offices of those who accompanied him, his imprisonment was not severe, and he was allowed every liberty to preach the gospel. From the soldiers it spread to the palace of the Cæsars, and ere long the Christians became so numerous as to attract the attention of the authorities. The gospel proved itself the power of God to salvation, and many of the Roman Christians sealed their testimony with their blood. Their blood became the seed of the Church. The gospel influenced all classes, and ere many years passed, Rome, the mistress of the world, bowed in lowly adoration before the Crucified, and on the spot where Paul died for his Master there now stands one of the most beautiful of the many Christian churches which form the glory and honour of modern Rome.

VI

THE GOSPEL IN THE EPISTLE TO THE PHILIPPIANS

WHEN Paul found himself on the shores of Troy, looking across the Ægean Sea, many thoughts must have been stirred within him. The whole neighbourhood possessed an undying interest. It was the scene of the Trojan war. It was not, however, of Troy that Paul was thinking, but of the regions beyond. It was not the heroes of the past that stood out before him, but the inhabitants of Greece sunk in sin and superstition, for whom he had a message of salvation and hope. Out of the darkness came a wailing cry, "Come over into Macedonia, and help us" (Acts xvi. 9). And his spirit had no rest until he responded to the cry and stood on the other side—the first to plant the standard of the Cross on the shores of Greece. What indomitable courage! What high-souled faith! A poor working Jew, not destitute of gifts, but belonging to a race everywhere despised, he never doubted the success of his mission. There was a splendid optimism about the Apostle

Paul. The gospel had proved a power to salvation in his own case. What it had done for him it could do for the whole race. It was bound to triumph. Jesus was the ascended and conquering Christ, to whom every knee should yet bow.

Following the highway from Neapolis, the Apostle soon found himself in the Roman colony of Philippi. Who was likely to receive him? Who would entertain this Jewish stranger, or listen to the message he was burning to deliver? By the riverside he found a little company of devout women who were accustomed to meet there on the Sabbath day for prayer and meditation, and with them he made friends. One of these women, named Lydia, was deeply moved by the story of the Crucified, and she forthwith opened her house to the Apostle and showed him every possible kindness. He soon had a larger audience; the testimony of the poor girl whom he restored to her right mind was, "These men are servants of the Most High God, which proclaim unto you the way of salvation" (Acts xvi. 17), a very concise definition of Paul's gospel. Although Paul's work in that city was somewhat rudely and abruptly terminated by the conduct of the authorities, it lasted long enough to leave permanent results. A little Church was formed there, whose members were distinguished for their faith and zeal in the cause of the gospel and for their tender and affectionate interest in the Apostle, manifested by many a kind gift to him. In fact it was the only Church that contributed to his maintenance or from which he would receive any contribution for himself (Phil. iv. 15). So close was Paul's relation with this Church that he not only received its gifts, but encouraged its members to cultivate such a generous spirit. Years passed away since his first visit, and the Apostle's mission carried him far and wide, but the Philippians were never forgotten. He had found his ambition gratified, to preach the gospel at Rome; but he had entered the imperial city as a prisoner of Jesus Christ, sent for trial before the emperor, who at that time was the inhuman Nero. His imprisonment, as we learn from the Acts of the Apostles, was not rigorous; considerable freedom was allowed to him, and he had many opportunities of preaching the gospel in Rome. Through some of the soldiers who were chained to him it seems to have found its way into the palace of the Cæsars. True, some were jealous of his success, and in no friendly spirit sought to outdo it; but this caused the Apostle no heart-burning. Whatever the motive of the preachers might be, the gospel was being proclaimed in Rome, and the name of Christ was being magnified in that city. Then, it would appear, there was a change in his treatment, and Paul's liberty was somewhat curtailed. He suffered, too, from want, for the Roman Christians were either not able or not disposed to succour him in his prison, and somehow or other the Philippians had been rather remiss in supplying his need (iv. 10). At last, however, there entered his prison a messenger from Philippi with good tidings of the spiritual condition of the Church there, and with the most opportune gifts from his friends. To thank them for this considerate kindness, he sent back the messenger, bearing with him the letter known as the Epistle to the Philippians, the first of the series written during his first imprisonment. It has been called a letter of thanks, a kindly letter drawn from the grateful heart of the Apostle.

In such a letter we do not look for elaborate statements of the gospel or formal dogmatic teaching. At the same time we have no difficulty in discovering from this letter the nature and contents of the gospel Paul had preached at Philippi, and in recognising its identity with that proclaimed in the Churches of Galatia and Corinth, and embodied in the Epistle to the Romans. He was filled with joy to know that Christ had been preached at Philippi, and we have seen what Paul meant by the preaching of Christ. It was the redemption of sinful men by the atoning death of Jesus Christ. It is recorded in the Acts of the Apostles that Paul's answer to the eager question of the Philippian jailor, "What must I do to be saved?" was, "Believe on the Lord Jesus, and thou shalt be saved" (Acts xvi. 30, 31). It was Jesus Christ and Him crucified that Paul pressed on the Philippians as the only way of salvation.

Besides these more general terms, we have in this Epistle one of the fullest statements regarding the person and work of Jesus to be found in the whole of Paul's writings. I refer to the remarkable passage in chap. ii. 6–11. It was the gospel of a Divine Saviour Paul presented to the Philippians as alone adequate to the wants of man. He knew, from his own deep experience, that deliverance from sin could come from no human source. It must come from God. And so the Saviour whom he offered, Jesus of Nazareth, born at Bethlehem, brought up at Nazareth, personally known to many of his countrymen, was Himself divine. His birth in Bethlehem was not the beginning of His existence. It was only its beginning under human conditions. "Who, being in the form of God, counted it not a prize to be equal with God" (ii. 6), terms which in Paul's mind seem to include the perfect Godhead of the Son. He takes the same view of Jesus as the author of the Fourth Gospel, the view evidently held by the first disciples. There Jesus is "the Word who was with God, who was God" (John i. 1), and who claimed for Himself equality with the Father (John x. 30). Being thus divine, He possessed the first great qualification for man's salvation. And how did the Divine Saviour carry out His work? Was it simply by the fiat of His own will proclaiming a free pardon to the guilty and reducing the sentence of death passed upon the race? That at least was not Paul's gospel. The salvation of fallen man involved an infinite sacrifice on His part, and so He laid aside all His glory and honour; He left the bosom of the Father and entered this world by the gate of birth, not as one of the great and honoured of the earth, but in the form of a servant who had come to minister to the wants of His fellow-men. "He emptied

Himself, taking the form of a servant, being made in the likeness of men" (ii. 7). And all this was but a means to a higher end, or, as the Apostle puts it, a lower step. He was made in the likeness of men, that He might pass through their experience, that He might for Himself as man discharge His obligations to the law, and having done so might suffer the death which the law declared to be the penalty of man's offence. "Being found in fashion as a man, He humbled Himself, becoming obedient even unto death" (ii. 8). To a lower depth even yet Jesus stooped. That one who "thought it not a prize to be on equality with God" should die was humbling in itself, but the death to which He submitted was the most painful and the most shameful. It was the death of the Cross. We have seen what the Cross of Jesus meant to Paul, so that in this passage the mystery of salvation is opened up; God incarnate dying by a shameful death at the hand of His creatures that He might extend His pardon to them, and so might reconcile them again to Himself. To the Philippians as to the Corinthians, Christ and Him crucified was the great theme of the gospel he proclaimed.

In the Gospel of Luke Jesus in His last words to His disciples is represented as instructing them: "That the Christ should suffer, and rise again from the dead the third day; and that repentance and remission of sins should be preached in His name unto all the nations" (Luke xxiv. 46, 47). Paul's gospel contained this truth. He knew well that the gospel of a dead Saviour alone could do little for the human race. The work of salvation was not finished when Jesus gave up the ghost and was laid in Joseph's tomb. It will not be finished until He puts all His enemies under His feet and presents each one of His people to the Father without blemish. The body of Jesus, laid in the grave, was not suffered to see corruption. It was raised from the dead, and in due time exalted by God to His own right hand. Jesus, crucified as a malefactor, has received the highest honour Heaven could award Him. His name is exalted above every name. It did not seem so when Paul wrote these words. The cultured Greek and the proud Roman scarcely knew the name. But Paul was an optimist. He believed in the Name. He knew the music, the magic, the miracle of the Name, and he saw with prophetic foresight that the time was coming when it would be everywhere honoured. " God highly exalted Him, and gave unto Him the name which is above every name; that in the name of Jesus every knee should bow, of things in heaven, and things on earth, and things under the earth; and that every tongue should confess that Jesus Christ is Lord, to the glory of God the Father" (ii. 8–11).

In the Epistles to the Galatians and the Romans, as we have seen, Paul vehemently insisted on the free justification of the sinner by divine grace. He set himself to break down the scaffolding of self-righteousness which some were seeking to erect around the work of Christ. The same theme is insisted on in this Epistle. He bids the Philippians beware of those who were seeking to establish a righteousness of their own. If a righteous man had ever lived on earth, he once thought that he was the man, and he puts forth his claim in most eulogistic terms, only however to throw contempt upon it. His excellences and advantages which, from a human standpoint, were unsurpassed, turned out to be utterly worthless from the divine. "What things were gain to me, these have I counted loss for Christ. Yea verily, and I count all things to be loss for the excellency of the knowledge of Christ Jesus my Lord: for whom I suffered the loss of all things, and do count them but dung, that I may gain Christ, and be found in Him, not having a righteousness of mine own, even that which is of the law, but that which is through faith in Christ, the righteousness which is of God by faith" (iii. 7–9). The words are an echo of Romans iii. 21, 22, and yet Godet points out that this very passage has been used by Holstein to prove that this Epistle could not have been written by Paul. "Paul would never have represented the Christian doctrine of justification as it is put in Phil. iii. 2–14, where it is made to consist in the progress of the knowledge of Christ in the heart of the believer. The justification taught by Paul is based upon the objective righteousness of Christ Himself."[1] But if one truth is more clearly taught than another by this passage, it is that the justification of the sinner rests on the righteousness

[1] Quoted by Godet, *Studies in the Epistles*, p. 260.

of another. It is through Christ that a righteousness of God is provided and received by faith.

Christ in His death had, according to Paul, one great end in view. It was not merely to seal His testimony with His blood that Jesus died. It was not merely as a sublime act of self-sacrifice for the sake of others. It was not merely to indicate His absolute surrender of Himself to the will of God, but it was to provide for man that righteousness to which he never could have attained by any efforts of his own. This was the truth that brought light to his own mind, as he had striven with intense earnestness to render acceptable service to God; and his heart failed him when he discovered how worthless his past life had been, and how he stood condemned before God. Then came the revelation of the gospel to him, the perfect righteousness of Jesus Christ, which became his through faith uniting him to Christ as his Saviour. From that moment he found peace with God. Not that he meant to say that he was perfect, but he was going on slowly and surely to that perfect ideal realised in the humiliation and exaltation of Jesus Christ.

Another characteristic of the gospel in this Epistle was the hope it inspired. Paul had boasted once that he was a citizen of no mean city. He now recognised a nobler citizenship to which all Christians belonged, but for whose investiture they had to wait for the coming again of the Saviour, the Lord Jesus Christ. That coming might not take place in their time, but it was certain Jesus would be manifested again, would touch the sleeping dust of His people, remould it into the likeness of His own body of glory, and raise each one of His servants to the honour of His Father's right hand. The gospel of Jesus Christ did not do much in bettering the outward condition of the Philippian Christians, though it has been the moving spirit in all the great social reformations in the world. It could, however, fill their hearts with a spirit of profound peace and contentment, and could inspire them with the hope of the inheritance with which they would be fully invested at the coming of Christ.

There is a note of joy running through the gospel of Paul, as there was in the message of the Saviour. Jesus was ever and anon calling upon His disciples to rejoice. His last conversations with them before His death had this in view, "that My joy may be in you, and that your joy may be fulfilled" (John xv. 11). For the gospel is glad tidings, and wherever it is accepted it brings the joy of pardon and of purity. And nothing was more characteristic of the early Christians than this spirit of joy. For the most part poor in worldly goods, exposed to reproach, persecution, and even death, they carried music in their hearts. So is it in this Epistle. We may apply to it what Dr. Martineau says of the Epistles of Paul generally: "Beneath the form of their theosophic reasonings, and their hints of deep philosophy, there may be heard a secret lyric strain of glorious praise, bursting at times into open utterance, and asking others to join in chorus, 'Rejoice in the Lord always; and again I say unto you, rejoice!'" (*Hours of Thought*, i. 156). The Apostle's joy was increased by two thoughts inspired by the gospel; the one was the conviction of the all-prevailing strength of Jesus made perfect in His people, assuring them of final triumph: " I can do all things in Him that strengtheneth me" (iv. 13). The other was the conviction that in Christ there was the fullest satisfaction of every want: "My God shall supply every need of yours according to His riches in glory in Christ Jesus." No wonder the Cross is associated with song. Jesus died, Jesus rose again. The fellowship of His sufferings and the power of His resurrection, —in these two truths you have the gospel in the Epistle to the Philippians.

VII

THE GOSPEL IN THE EPISTLE TO THE COLOSSIANS

THE first imprisonment of Paul at Rome was one of the most fruitful periods of his ministry. He was, in a sense, under the imperial protection, safe from the intrigues of his enemies, and allowed considerable liberty in preaching to the Gentiles the unsearchable riches of Christ. He greatly rejoiced at the success attending the gospel in Rome, for he could scarcely foresee the attempt soon to be made to exterminate the Christians throughout the empire. To his prison came messengers from the Churches he had founded, bringing to him tidings of their spiritual condition, and often carrying back with them letters in which the Apostle sought to instruct the Churches more fully in the faith once delivered to the saints, to warn them against false teachers, and to exhort them to steadfast continuance in the Christian life.

Amongst those who thus visited him were two members of the Church at Colossæ. One was a runaway slave whom he sent back to his master with a letter in which he bespoke for him a kindly reception and treatment; the other was a faithful teacher called Epaphras, the founder, as many have thought, of the Colossian Church. He had much to tell Paul of his experiences in that city. He had an encouraging report to give of the faith and love and prayers of the Colossian Christians (i. 4–8). But he had also to report the arrival of false teachers who were seeking to beguile the converts from the simple gospel of Jesus Christ, and to confuse their minds with certain mystic teachings about light and darkness, matter and spirit, good and evil, angels and spiritual powers, and to bring them into bondage to ordinances and rites from which they had been delivered by the truth as it was in Jesus (ii. 4, 8, 20, 21). The manifest tendency of this system of error which had found its way into Colossæ was to detract from the supreme honour and glory of the Lord Jesus Christ. These tidings caused sorrow of heart to the Apostle in his imprisonment, and he wrote a letter to the members of the Colossian Church, or perhaps we should say Churches, which he sent by the hands of Epaphras, a letter in which praise and blame are skilfully blended. Paul was a stranger to these Churches. His language seems to indicate that he had never visited them (ii. 1). All he knew of them was by hearsay, and this had favourably impressed him. He was anxious that nothing should efface this good impression or in any way injure their Christian standing. There is no angry recrimination in this letter. The

Apostle pursues a more excellent way. He recalls them to the gospel which had been proclaimed among them. He reminds them that it was the gospel of the Lord Jesus Christ, in which emphasis was laid on His person and work. He reminds them of the freedom from old forms and ceremonies enjoyed under the gospel dispensation, and of the glorious end contemplated by the gospel, the restoration of the whole creation to that original state of purity and perfection enjoyed when it was called into existence by Jesus Christ. As we read this Epistle we recognise in it the same gospel in which Paul always gloried. It is the gospel of Jesus Christ the Lord; the gospel of Him who, though the Creator of all things, had stooped to the death of the Cross, that He might reconcile all things to Himself, and through whom was offered to men the forgiveness of their sin; the gospel of Him who was the risen and ascended Saviour, and who was destined to subdue all things to Himself.

In this presentation of the gospel, the first thing that claims our attention is, the exalted position assigned by Paul to Jesus Christ. The Eastern mind was greatly exercised with the problem of good and evil, and gave birth to many ingenious and idle speculations bearing on the problem. One of these was, that matter was essentially evil, and owed its origin to a being who was in direct opposition to the God of light and truth. In this theory men found an apology for sin, and so their sense of responsibility was weakened. Creation, according to this view, was peopled with innumerable spirits exercising their influence over men and carrying on an incessant conflict with the powers of light and goodness. To all this the Apostle opposed the one manifestation which the Supreme Being had been pleased to make of Himself in the person of the Lord Jesus Christ. The Saviour the gospel offered for their acceptance was "the image of the invisible God," existing before the whole creation, Himself the Creator, the agent of God the Father in this mighty work, to whom all powers and principalities and angels owed their existence, and by whom alone they are continued in being (ii. 13–16). With the Eternal Son of God no creature can compare. He stands above them all, possessing in Himself the treasures of wisdom and knowledge, "in whom it was the good pleasure of the Father that all the fulness should dwell" (i. 18, 19). If men needed a mediator to come between the Father and them, he was no angelic spirit, no heavenly power, by whatever name he might be called. God had provided this Mediator in the person of His own Son on whom He had put such distinguished honour, and whom He besought the Colossians not to dethrone from His high position by putting in His place any creature offered to them by a vain philosophy (ii. 20–23).

Now, no doubt, this is a deeper and more profound view of Jesus Christ than is presented in the earlier writings of the Apostle, though it is only the rational expansion of his teaching regarding the person of Jesus contained in them. In the

Epistle to the Philippians he had spoken of the pre-existent glory of Jesus Christ and of the place to which at His resurrection He had been exalted by God the Father. He had spoken of Him as the Son of God with power (Rom. i. 4). Repeatedly in the Epistles to the Corinthians He is called the Lord Jesus Christ, while His mediatorial position in heaven forms part of the teaching of I. Cor. xv. Here, however, Jesus is placed at the beginning of all things, the Head of the creation, Himself before all things, and therefore uncreated. There can be little doubt that Paul in this Epistle was combating the same error with which the Beloved Disciple was confronted, and so his language and thought remind us of the Fourth Gospel. His gospel of the eternal and incarnate Son of God resembles that of the gospel of John. Jesus is the one Being in the universe who in all things has the pre-eminence.[1]

The second thing to be noticed in Paul's presentation of his gospel to the Colossian Christians is the manner in which he refers to the work and mission of Jesus Christ. The gospel had been preached to them by his messengers in the terms

[1] "We know comparatively little of the sect of the Essenes; but we are sure that the mediation and worship of angels were prominent features of their religious system, and that the ideal of life which they practised was modelled on the spirituality of angelic intelligences. . . . Once assume that a leaven of that kind had invaded the Churches on the Lycus, and we shall have a sufficient explanation of the emphasis placed on the higher aspects of Christ's person and work" (Dr. Somerville, *St. Paul's Conception of Christ*, p. 153).

in which he himself was in the habit of presenting it. The Gentile world had been long held in the bondage of darkness and superstition by the god of this world. Jesus had come to deliver men from all this, to render them dissatisfied with their darkness and ignorance. He had come to make them restless in their sin and guilt and condemnation. He had come to show them the way of salvation through Himself, and to translate them into the kingdom of God's dear Son (i. 13). He had effected this by paying a price for them. "In whom we have our redemption" (i. 14), *i.e.* deliverance obtained by paying a price. In the parallel passage in Eph. i. 7, the words "through His blood" are added, and though these are omitted by the Revisers in this passage, we cannot doubt that the thought was present to the mind of the Apostle,—"the reference being to redemption from the wrath and punitive justice of God in its most comprehensive signification."[1] And this redemption the Apostle identifies with "the forgiveness of our sins." For it is to sin we must trace the separation of man from God, the darkening of the mind, the hardening of the heart, and the corruption of the nature. So that all spiritual life and light and joy depend on the forgiveness of our sin, and this we have in Christ, whose high qualifications to forgive sin the Apostle goes on to enumerate. For the work of Christ is also that of the Reconciler who, in some profound sense, brings the whole created universe into a state of recon-

[1] Ellicott, *in loco.*

ciliation with God the Father (i. 19–22). Men are not only the subjects of the kingdom of darkness, they are also "alienated and enemies in their mind by their evil works." There are some who tell us that the human race emerged from a condition of barbarism and has been steadily advancing on an ever-ascending path; but it is difficult to reconcile the statement with the word of God. Instead of beginning with the ascent of man, it begins with his descent. Scripture reminds us that whereas "God made men upright, they have sought out many inventions," that whereas man was God's child whom He nourished and brought up, he has rebelled against Him. Instead of loving God, he has come to be afraid of Him and to be estranged from Him. Worse than that, he has even entertained a hostile feeling toward God, which has found expression in a life of sin. And this enmity has provoked the divine displeasure, and induced the breach between God and man. Now Jesus Christ has come to destroy the enmity. He has come as the reconciler to bring us once more near to God, and for that purpose it was necessary that He should come in "a body of flesh." For on the truth of the human nature of Christ the Apostle was as emphatic as on that of His divine nature. "He would point the contrast between the divine dignity of the eternal Word, the Creator and Lord of the universe, and the lowliness of His incarnation. On these two pillars, as on two solid piers, one on either continent, with a great gulf between, the divinity of Christ on one side, His manhood on the other, is built this bridge by which we pass over the river into glory." [1]

In Paul's view the incarnation was not sufficient in itself to effect the reconciliation; there must be the death of the Son of God "in the body of His flesh through death." It is on the ground of what Christ did when He died for man that the Apostle rests this reconciliation. We may not be able to define how this is effected. But the language of the Apostle is plain, that it removes some obstacle in the way of God as well as of man. Jesus takes the nature of sinful man, renders a perfect obedience to the law of God, and dies the innocent for the guilty. This at least is Paul's teaching, the gospel of the grace of God revealed to him, and he had come to know the power of the gospel in overcoming the enmity of the human heart. It is the revelation of the Father's love in the gift of His Son, the revelation of the love of the Son in giving Himself up to death, that breaks down the sinner's enmity, and lays him low at the feet of the Crucified.

This reconciliation is spoken of under another figure often used by the Apostle Paul. The Colossians before they received the gospel were dead in trespasses and sins; the law had pronounced its sentence upon them; they were condemned. And they were dead, inasmuch as they were completely under the dominion of sin. Now Jesus had come as the life-giver, and the life bestowed by Him consisted in forgiving men their trespasses. The convict

---

[1] Maclaren, *Expositor's Bible*, "Colossians."

upon whom the law has pronounced sentence of death is from that moment as good as dead. He has lost all the rights of a living man. He has no standing in society or before the law. But if mercy is extended to him, if he has a free pardon put into his hand, if his sentence is cancelled, then his position becomes altered; he is no longer dead in the eyes of the law. His property is restored to him, he is put in possession of his rights. This is the position of the sinner under the gospel. So long as the law stood over against him, demanding perfect obedience, and death for failing to render it, he was under the bondage of fear. But now Jesus Christ has come, "having forgiven us all our trespasses; having blotted out the handwriting of ordinances that was against us, which was contrary to us; and He hath taken it out of the way, nailing it to the cross" (ii. 13, 14). It is in the Cross Paul glories. There it stands, the instrument of death, but on the Cross Jesus triumphed over all His enemies, especially over all those spiritual powers which had been holding men in subjection. The Cross meant the death of sin, the defeat of the god of this world, the victory over death itself (ii. 15). To the Colossians that meant their complete deliverance from the law of ordinances and from that ritual into which some were trying to bring them again into bondage. Knowledge and belief of the truth as it is in Jesus made them free.

In the Epistle to the Colossians, as in all his other letters, Paul dwells on the moral contents of his gospel. The great end of the reconciling work of Christ was not simply to destroy our enmity, was not merely to bring to us the forgiveness of sin, but was to make this an end to the victory over sin and sinful habit: " You hath He reconciled in the body of His flesh through death, to present you holy and without blemish and unreproveable before Him" (i. 22). " Christ whom we proclaim . . . that we may present every man perfect in Christ" (i. 27, 28). This is the ultimate end of the work and mission of Jesus Christ, the reconciliation of all things unto God, the restoration throughout the universe of the perfect harmony, disturbed by the entrance of sin. How this is to be brought about is one of the secret things which belong unto the Lord, but the fact of its accomplishment is more than once hinted at by the Apostle. One of the means towards this great end is the complete sanctification of the individual believer, the realisation of the presence and love of Jesus Christ in all the relations and duties of this present life. Jesus the Crucified is also Jesus the risen Saviour, who has taken to Himself His new and glorified life. The faith of the believer makes him one with the risen as well as with the dead Christ. He ought therefore to " seek the things which are above, where Christ is seated on the right hand of God, to set his mind on the things that are above, not on the things that are on the earth " (iii. 1, 2). The believer does not now live for this world. He has been crucified to it. He is dead to those things which constitute the life of the world, and the life he now lives is on a higher plane: "For ye died, and your life is hid with Christ in God." It is really Christ's life maintained by faith which keeps the believer in abiding union with Him. But one day Jesus shall come again and be manifested to the eyes of men. The Saviour who was crucified, who was raised from the dead to the right hand of God, shall appear in the glory of His Father and of the holy angels, the crowned King of the universe, and with Him shall be manifested all His people in glory.

VIII

THE GOSPEL IN THE EPISTLE TO THE EPHESIANS

BETWEEN the Epistle to the Ephesians and the Epistle to the Colossians there is a very striking resemblance, so much so that some have come to the conclusion that it is only an expanded form of the letter to the Colossian Churches. In the opinion of others it is identified with the epistle from Laodicea, which Paul was anxious should be read and studied at Colossæ, and various reasons have been urged for this view. There are no personal greetings in the letter, such as might have been expected in a communication addressed to a Church founded by the Apostle, and in which he had laboured for a long period. It has also been said that various expressions appear to indicate that Paul was not personally acquainted with the members of the Church to whom he was writing. Not much stress can be put upon this last statement, as the expressions referred to are not incompatible with the Apostle's acquaintance with the Ephesian Christians. On the other hand, as

EPISTLE TO THE EPHESIANS

we saw, it would have been strange if Paul had not sent any written communication to the Churches of Galatia; it would have been even stranger if he had not done so to the Church at Ephesus. The very affectionate terms in which he addresses the members of the Church seem to imply personal acquaintance with them; and above all the subject-matter of the Epistle is quite in keeping with what we know of the social, intellectual, and religious state of Ephesus at the time of Paul's visit. At the same time it is quite probable that, "if addressed primarily to the Christians at Ephesus, it was still designed for all the Churches conterminous to or dependent on that city." [1]

Paul had paid a brief visit to Ephesus after leaving Corinth, but on that occasion he had confined his labours to his own countrymen. On his return from Jerusalem he made a longer visit there, and boldly attacked heathenism. Ephesus was at that time the meeting-place of the East and the West, as Smyrna is at the present day. The wealth of Europe and Asia poured into its markets, making it the "Vanity Fair of Asia." [2] The variety of races represented there, and the activity and wealth of its traders, made Ephesus an important centre for the diffusion of Christian ideas. At the time of his visit Ephesus was the seat of an idolatrous cult, which had made it famous throughout the world, and which stirred

---

[1] Ellicott's *Commentary*, Introduction.
[2] Farrar, *St. Paul*.

the fighting spirit in the Apostle. He saw there heathenism in its more revolting forms. "It was an almost theocratic town; the fêtes there were numerous and splendid; the right wing of the temple peopled the town with courtesans. The scandalous sacerdotal institutions maintained there appeared each day devoid of all shame."[1] Instead of the philosophic spirit that prevailed in Athens, Paul found himself face to face with the grossest superstition. "The town swarmed with magicians, diviners, mummers, and flute players; eunuchs, jewellers, sellers of amulets and medals, and romancers."[2]

From his lodging in the city, and from the school of one Tyrannus, Paul began his attack on the superstition, the scandalous idolatries, and the loose lives of the Ephesians, and preached to them the word of the Lord Jesus. In his farewell address to the elders of Ephesus, Paul reminded them how for nearly three years he had preached to them "repentance toward God, and faith toward our Lord Jesus Christ (Acts xx. 21). The result of these labours was the formation of a vigorous Christian Church in Ephesus, a Church that long continued to be one of the most active centres of Christian influence, and was at a later period the scene of the labours of the Apostle John. Paul felt a strong attachment to his converts in this heathen city, and when his long imprisonment in Rome gave him ample leisure for correspondence, he wrote to them a

[1] Renan, *St. Paul*.   [2] *Ibid.*

letter in which we can still read his warm love for the Ephesian converts, and the great joy he had in their Christian standing and progress. In this Epistle he presents them with a new view of the gospel, likely to commend it to their minds, while it contains the same leading truths on which his other letters insisted. In lofty and impassioned language he treats of the highest mysteries; he strikes a note of jubilant praise, while he condescends to the utmost plainness of speech in dealing with the most practical subjects. It is "a creed soaring into the loftiest of evangelic psalms."[1]

The main theme of the Epistle is "the calling to salvation by grace, addressed as freely to the Gentiles as to the Jews."[2] But here in his presentation of the gospel Paul has something new to say of it. It is in the Epistle to the Ephesians that *he traces salvation to its origin*. He had indeed hinted at this sublime conception in the Epistles to the Thessalonians (II. Thess. iv. 7, v. 9; 2 Thess. ii. 13) and in the Epistle to the Romans. Here he gives full expression to it. Like the Apostle of Love, he has looked into the unseen and inscrutable counsels of God the Father. The Apostle John tells us that the angel who initiated him into the mystery of the city of God showed him "a river of water of life, ... proceeding out of the throne of God and of the Lamb" (Rev. xxii. 1). But Paul has an even more exalted view of

[1] Farrar, *St. Paul*, ii. p. 48.
[2] Godet, *Studies in the Epistles*, p. 210.

salvation. He traces it back to its source not in space only but also in time. In the Epistle to the Romans the Apostle asserted that salvation was not confined to the Jews, inasmuch as its blessings were promised to Abraham previous to the divine covenant with him as the head of the nation; but here he discloses that from all eternity the plan of God the Father embraced the human race, and His infinite wisdom conceived the plan that was fully carried out in the mission and death of His Son, and shall be gloriously consummated in the final glory of man along with his exalted Redeemer (Eph. i. 3–14). The ruin of the human race was foreseen by the Divine Being long ere it was called into existence, and so also was the mission and death of His Son, who undertook to become incarnate in the fulness of the time, and to do the will of the Father. One of Paul's noblest conceptions of the gospel to which he had given expression in the Epistle to the Colossians (Col. i. 18–22) is repeated in this Epistle, that the whole universe was to be brought into final harmony with God Himself through Jesus Christ His Son (Eph. i. 10). So that we have not only the sublime origin of the gospel stated in this Epistle, but also its far-reaching and glorious aim. And in this presentation of the gospel the design of the Apostle is to excite our admiration of the divine goodness and grace, by tracing the salvation of the race entirely to the love of the Divine Father.

This view of the gospel brings into greater

prominence ITS UNIVERSALITY. If the divine plan of salvation embraced the race, it must have been before the Jewish nation existed. It was salvation for the race and not for a nation, though the knowledge and enjoyment of it were long the privilege of the Jews. And this truth, so worthy of universal acceptance and belief, had long been a mystery, concealed from the world up to gospel times. It was indeed foreshadowed, as the Apostle tells us in some of his other Epistles, both in patriarchal and Jewish promises, but it had not been clearly made manifest, as it had since been by Jesus Christ, and especially by his own call to preach unto the Gentiles the unsearchable riches of Christ (Eph. iii. 1–12). It was a view of the gospel likely to take in Ephesus, for the Ephesians were fond of mysteries, and here was the mystery of mysteries on which to concentrate all their powers of mind, a mystery hid from the ages, "that the Gentiles are fellow-heirs, and fellow-members of the body, and fellow-partakers of the promise in Christ Jesus through the gospel" (Eph. iii. 6).

Again, in this Epistle the gospel is viewed as SALVATION BY GRACE. It traces man's salvation entirely to the divine grace, mercy, or love. It dates from eternity, and so cannot concern itself with the personal merit of the individual saved. It is all of grace. "Having in love foreordained us" (Eph. i. 4, R.V. margin), "according to the good pleasure of His will" (i. 6). "God being rich in mercy, for His great love wherewith He loved us, even when we were dead in our trespasses, quickened us together with Christ (by grace have ye been saved). . . . That in the ages to come He might shew the exceeding riches of His grace in kindness toward us in Christ Jesus" (ii. 4–7). The saved sinner has nothing whereof to boast; he is a trophy of divine grace. He joins his voice with that of the whole redeemed creation in singing the praises of the Redeemer's glory. "By grace are ye saved through faith; and that not of yourselves: it is the gift of God; not of works, lest any man should boast" (ii. 8, 9). As the Apostle dwells on the grace of God his language becomes more exalted —he does not know how to express himself. He can only desire for himself and all his converts "that Christ may dwell in your hearts through faith; to the end that ye, being rooted and grounded in love, may be strong to apprehend with all the saints what is the breadth and length and height and depth, and to know the love of Christ which passeth knowledge" (iii. 17–19).

If, indeed, there was one consideration more than another to bring into greater prominence this grace of God, it was the spiritual condition of the Ephesians when they first heard the word of the truth of the gospel, the gospel of their salvation. They were not in the happy position of the Jewish converts, to whom the law of God was well known, and who had been trying to live up to its requirements. "They were alienated from the commonwealth of Israel, and strangers from the covenants of the promise, having no hope and without God in the world" (ii. 12). "They were Gentiles in the flesh," "dead through their trespasses and sins, wherein they walked according to the course of this world, according to the prince of the power of the air, that now worketh in the sons of disobedience. . . . The children of wrath even as others" (ii. 2). They had walked "as the Gentiles also walked, in the vanity of their mind, being darkened in their understanding, alienated from the life of God because of the ignorance that is in them, because of the hardening of their hearts; who being past feeling gave themselves up to lasciviousness, to work all uncleanness with greediness" (iv. 17–19). The more therefore the Ephesians dwelt on their former condition, the more would they magnify the grace of God who had saved them and quickened them, and made them a new creation in Christ Jesus.

And this salvation the Apostle was careful to tell them was by the blood of Jesus Christ. Redemption through the blood of Christ and reconciliation by blood are the two saving truths of the gospel presented in this Epistle. The gospel is stated almost in the same terms as it was to the Colossians. It was to the death of Jesus Christ that they owed their deliverance from the guilt of sin; for pardon must precede purity, justification must precede though it carries with it sanctification. It is in the death of Christ that the sinner sees his guilt expiated and the sentence of condemnation cancelled. There, too, he sees the forgiveness of his sins. In the same way the sinner who is represented as standing afar off from God, separated by the barrier of a holy law which he has broken, sees the barrier taken out of the way by the death of Jesus, and so is brought nigh (ii. 13). The enmity due in a sense to the law is destroyed in His flesh, *i.e.* His crucified flesh (Ellicott, *in loco*), as reconciliation is effected in His body by the Cross on which the enmity has been slain (ii. 16). Thus Christ becomes what the Apostle calls "our Peace," and in Him is realised the angels' song "peace on earth." It is just another way of stating his gospel. The gospel to the Ephesians was a gospel of peace. They need no longer stand afar off with the fear of "strangers and sojourners," but may draw near with confidence "as fellow-citizens with the saints, and of the household of God." Thus again on Jesus Christ and the teaching of His Apostles, the temple of God, long in ruins, was being reconstructed, in which when completed God would take up His abode by His Spirit (ii. 19, 20).

Such was the gospel which had been preached in Ephesus, and which the Ephesians had heard. Paul had offered them a Saviour. They had believed His message and trusted the Saviour. It was their faith in Jesus that had so changed them. For it brought to them the indwelling of the Holy Spirit, sealing them as heirs of the inheritance, witnessing to their adoption into the family of God. "In whom ye also, having heard the word of the truth, the gospel of your salvation,—in whom, having also believed, ye were sealed with the Holy Spirit of promise" (i. 13, 14).

The gospel presented to the Ephesians was also a practical gospel. This is the burden of the three last chapters. Paul preached deliverance from guilt by the death of Jesus, he preached also deliverance from sin. The divine plan contemplated a renewed creation, and this purpose was being realised in time. God chose them and called them to be holy (i. 4). They "were created in Christ Jesus for good works, which God afore prepared that we should walk in them" (ii. 10). The redeemed man must "put on the new man, which after God hath been created in righteousness and holiness of truth" (iv. 24). He must put away from him all lying and wrath, all covetous desires and impure thoughts, all vain and foolish talk, all malice, and must walk as a child of the light, bringing forth "the fruit of the Spirit in all goodness and righteousness and truth." The Apostle further carries this thought of the new creation in Christ Jesus into all the relations of life, of husband and wife, of parent and child, of master and servant, and urges the Ephesian Christians in all these relations to act as those who have been redeemed by Christ, and are bound to conduct themselves as followers or imitators of Christ.

Finally, he reminds them that the gospel he preached to them was a gospel of conflict and victory. He knew what a struggle these converts from the darkness and superstition and abominations of paganism would have to come through ere they were enabled by the grace of God to gain the victory over their old habits and manner of life.

He knew the temptations by which they were assailed, the vigilance and cunning of their spiritual foes, and he reminded them that the Saviour who had brought to them His great salvation had also sought to arm them for the conflict. To succeed in this great fight they must live near to Christ, must be always on the alert, sending up their prayers to Him for His promised help and strength. Thus in the fulness of the time the glorious plan of God would be consummated, and the redeemed creation renewed again into the image of Jesus Christ would form the body of Him who is exalted, "far above all rule, and authority, and power, and dominion, and every name that is named, not only in this world, but also in that which is to come: . . . to be head of the Church, which is His body, the fulness of Him that filleth all in all" (i. 21–23).

IX

THE GOSPEL IN THE EPISTLES TO TIMOTHY

THE Epistles to Timothy and Titus form what have been called the Pastoral Epistles, and are supposed to have been written in the interval between the first and second imprisonments of Paul at Rome, one at least shortly before his martyrdom. Their genuineness, though almost universally accepted during the second century, has been called in question in this, because of the marked difference in style, in subjects, and in the treatment of these subjects. But when we bear in mind that they are the letters of a man prematurely old, to some of his dearest friends, written almost on the brink of the grave, it is easy to understand that he would take for granted their familiarity with the main truths of his teaching, and would be more anxious to provide for the future care of the Churches in which he was so deeply interested. At the same time we are continually coming across Pauline phrases and thoughts in these Epistles. "Pauline in much of their phraseology,

Pauline in their fundamental doctrines, Pauline in their dignity and holiness of tone, Pauline alike in their tenderness and severity, Pauline in the digressions, the constructions, and the personality of their style, we may accept two of them with an absolute conviction of their authenticity; and the third—the First Epistle to Timothy, which is more open to doubt than the others—with at least a strong belief that in reading it we are reading the words of the greatest of the Apostles."[1] The first two Epistles bear to be written to Timothy, whom the writer calls in the first "my true child in faith" (I. i. 2), and in the second "my beloved child" (II. i. 2), both of which terms very appropriately describe the relation in which Timothy stood to the Apostle. From his first meeting with Timothy at Lystra, Paul's heart went out to the lad, who returned the affection of the older man. When an unhappy strife had separated Paul from Barnabas, his companion in his first missionary journey, he drew to Timothy, who after a time became his close and trusted companion. He was with him in many of his travels, was employed on confidential missions, inquiring into the spiritual state of the Churches, combating errors, rebuking those whose conduct called for censure, taking the oversight of some of the most important Churches founded by his master, and was summoned to be his companion in his last imprisonment. It is impossible to affirm what length of time intervened between

[1] Farrar, *St. Paul*, ii. p. 622.

the first and second imprisonments of Paul. But we gather from the First Epistle that Timothy had been with the Apostle in Rome, and had accompanied him in a visit paid to the Churches of Greece and Asia Minor (I. i. 3). He had been left by the Apostle in charge of the Church at Ephesus, over which he was ordained as overseer (I. iv. 14). Paul had evidently heard of the presence of certain false teachers in Ephesus, and of the conduct of some of his converts, and so he addressed to his dear friend a letter overflowing with love, charging him to be faithful to the gospel committed to him, and providing for the proper oversight of the Church; and when he was again imprisoned, his heart yearned for Timothy, and having a presentiment that his death was near at hand, he besought Timothy in a second letter to come to Rome as quickly as possible, and to bring with him certain things of which he felt the want.

Such appears to be the origin of these Epistles, and so we are not likely to find in them such statements of the gospel as we find in the Epistles meant for the instruction of the Churches. Paul was writing to a devoted Christian worker, who had been well grounded in the Jewish Scriptures by his grandmother and his mother, and whom he had himself taken great pains to instruct in the truth as it is in Jesus, and to train for the work of the ministry. If anyone was likely to know Paul's gospel it was Timothy, so that we scarcely expect to find in these letters more than general allusions to the great subjects of the Apostle's teaching.

What we do find are earnest exhortations to Timothy to continue steadfast in the truths he had learned from his master, and not to be led away by the vain speculations of other teachers. With these are precious autobiographical notes, in which we get glimpses of the Apostle's life in Rome, and of his undying love to the Lord Jesus Christ.

Some critics indeed have said that the conception of the gospel in these letters differs notably from the well-known teaching of Paul, and that the prominence given to good works is inconsistent with the importance Paul elsewhere attaches to justification by faith. But in all the Epistles we have studied we have seen how he insisted on the ethical contents of faith. All the great leading features of his gospel are to be found in these letters, as matters with which Timothy was known to be quite familiar.

First of all Paul attaches the utmost importance to the gospel itself. He reminds his disciple that it was the gospel in which he had himself instructed him. He speaks of it as sound or healthful doctrine, sound words, calculated to benefit all who received and believed it, of which Timothy ought never to be ashamed (I. i. 10, 11, vi. 3; ii. 1, 8, 13). For in these days, as in our own, there is a strong tendency to turn away from sound doctrine and to seek after novelty. And then he calls it the "gospel of the glory of the blessed God" (I. i. 11), because it comes from the glory of the infinite and eternal Father. Jesus came from His bosom full of grace and truth, that men might see His glory. When the people heard the gospel from the lips of Jesus, they glorified God; and the Saviour's purpose in His sacrifice, death, resurrection, and ascension was to bring many sons to glory. The gospel had been committed to the Apostle's charge. To bear testimony to the gospel he had been appointed a preacher and an apostle and a teacher of the Gentiles in truth. It was an honour of which he felt himself utterly unworthy, considering what he had once been. He lifts the veil from his past life, and tells Timothy what he was before he knew the gospel. He had been a persecutor and a blasphemer of the name that was now dearest to him, and had sought to exterminate the followers of Jesus. But all this had been done in ignorance. He was acting up to his light and to his most sacred convictions, and God had mercy on him and had magnified His grace toward him. "Faithful is the saying, and worthy of all acceptation, that Christ Jesus came into the world to save sinners; of whom I am chief" (I. i. 15). It is the gospel in a sentence, the story of Jesus Christ mighty to save sinners, the echo of the words of Jesus: "The Son of Man came to seek and to save that which was lost" (Luke xix. 10). To this truth Paul was himself a living testimony. "Howbeit for this cause I obtained mercy, that in me as chief Jesus Christ might shew forth all His long-suffering, for an ensample of them which should hereafter believe on Him unto eternal life" (I. i. 16).

To this general statement of the gospel, Paul adds

several striking particulars. We recognise here, too, the truth on which we saw he had laid such great stress in the Epistle to the Ephesians, salvation by the grace of God: "The grace of our Lord abounded exceedingly with faith and love which is in Christ Jesus" (I. i. 4). "God saved us, and called us with an holy calling, not according to our works, but according to His own purpose and grace, which was given us in Christ Jesus before times eternal, but hath now been manifested by the appearing of our Saviour Christ Jesus" (II. i. 9, 10). It is part of Paul's gospel in these letters that for the purpose of effecting the salvation of the sinner the Son of God must become man, and so he says: "Christ Jesus came into the world" (I. i. 15); "He was manifested in the flesh" (I. iii. 16); He was "of the seed of David" (II. ii. 8); He was "the man Christ Jesus" (I. ii. 5). The Saviour was truly a man born into this world, who had lived a very human life, but He was at the same time our Lord Jesus Christ, our hope, our life.

Still further, Paul tells Timothy for what purpose the Son of God came into the world and was manifested in the flesh. It was "to save sinners," and it was to be "the one Mediator between God and man" (I. ii. 5). These are two ways of stating the same truth; the one views man as a sinner who has failed to keep the divine law and so incurred the divine displeasure; the other views man as having alienated himself from God and taken up a hostile attitude toward Him, and so as standing in need of reconciliation. The term Mediator is a new one as applied to Christ, but the idea is a Pauline one, with which the Epistles to the Corinthians and the Romans have made us familiar.[1] Reconciliation is necessary on the part both of God and man. There is an obstacle on God's side, so long as sin is unexpiated; there is an obstacle on man's side, arising from the state of his own heart. At the same time it is the divine love that has provided the Mediator who has come to take these out of the way. "God willeth that all men should be saved" (I. ii. 4); for only one combining in himself the natures of the divine and human, only one having the most perfect understanding of the purpose of God and of the condition of man, could take upon himself to act as mediator between the two parties. It was for this purpose that the Son of God became man, that He might be the one and only Mediator between God and man, that He might bring the two together, remove causes of offence, and reconcile them in a covenant of eternal peace. This is the gospel we have met with in the Epistles to the Ephesians and Colossians, where Jesus is spoken of as our Peace who has come to reconcile us to God.[2]

More, however, was needed to qualify Jesus Christ to act as Mediator than simply that He should become man. Jesus Himself had indicated that His incarnation was only one step in His redemptive

---

[1] Rom. v. 10; II. Cor. v. 18, 19.
[2] Eph. ii. 13, 14; Col. i. 20-22.

work, and the gospel of Paul is no less clear on this point, and so he immediately adds, "who gave Himself a ransom for all" (I. ii. 6). Here again the atoning death is placed by Paul in the very front of his gospel, and stated with singular clearness. The word for ransom here is a very strong term, occurring nowhere else in the New Testament. "In this important word, the idea of a substitution of Christ in our stead cannot be ignored, especially when connected with passages of such deep significance as Rom. iii. 25."[1] So complete was the alienation between God and man, that man might in truth be said to have sold himself into bondage, and his redemption could only be accomplished by paying the ransom price. That price was a life of such priceless value as could alone be accepted by God. That price none could pay but the Lord Jesus Christ, "who gave Himself a ransom for all." Or, to put it in another form, by paying the ransom price, He takes away a formidable obstacle to the reconciliation of God and man. "Man is ransomed from the disastrous state of punishment, in that the demand for his punishment is satisfied by the death of Christ as a vicarious sacrifice."[2]

In these Epistles, too, we have one precious little biographical detail of the historic Christ, namely, that "He before Pontius Pilate witnessed the good confession" (I. vi. 13), and sealed His testimony with His blood.

---

[1] Ellicott, *in loco*.
[2] Pfleiderer, *Paulinismus*, Eng. trans. i. p. 92.

The gospel, however, is more than a gospel of reconciliation or mediatorship. The work of Christ is far-reaching in its consequences. Jesus does more than atone for guilt. He is the destroyer of sin, and "He has abolished death, and brought life and incorruption to light through the gospel" (II. i. 10). We have "the promise of the life which is in Christ Jesus" (II. i. 1). By His appearing, which Bengel regards as the whole time of the abode of Christ among men, "He hath rendered of none effect death" as "a power or principle pervading and overshadowing the world."[1] For the gospel alone has taken the sting from death, and shed light on what comes after death. And Jesus has done so by His resurrection. "Remember Jesus Christ, risen from the dead" (II. ii. 2). "If we died with Him, we shall also live with Him" (II. ii. 11). It is a concise way of stating the truth which the Apostle had so fully expounded in the fifteenth chapter of the First Epistle to the Corinthians. The similarity of the teaching, as well of the language, goes far to prove that the author of the Epistles to Timothy is the same with the author of those we have already considered.

From these Epistles, too, we gather what Paul's teaching was regarding the work of Jesus Christ in the future state. The Saviour is to be manifested there as the "judge of the quick and the dead" (II. iv. 1). To this office His Father has exalted Him, and at His judgment-seat all flesh shall

[1] Ellicott, *in loco.*

appear. He bids Timothy keep his heart fixed on this appearing of the Lord Jesus Christ. This is our Saviour's own personal teaching, and it is clearly stated by the author of the Fourth Gospel. "Neither doth the Father judge any man, but He hath given all judgement unto the Son" (John v. 22). And it is the teaching of Paul in other Epistles. "We must all be made manifest before the judgement-seat of Christ" (II. Cor. v. 10). (See also Rom. xiv. 10, where, however, the R.V. reads "the judgement-seat of God.") By the aged Apostle this manifestation of Christ was eagerly anticipated. He had told the Philippians, when the issue of his first imprisonment was doubtful, that "he had the desire to depart and to be with Christ; for it is very far better" (Phil. i. 23). "To die is gain" (Phil. i. 21). And now when the clouds are gathering overhead and his prison door would open only to lead him to the martyr's death, he is quite calm, nay, even joyful. "I am already being offered, and the time of my departure is come. I have fought the good fight, I have finished the course, I have kept the faith: henceforth there is laid up for me the crown of righteousness, which the Lord, the righteous judge, shall give to me at that day" (II. iv. 6–8). It is no wonder that, with such a hope, Paul was never ashamed of the gospel. Perhaps nowhere does his faith shine forth so brightly as in the passage where he bears his testimony to the Saviour and to His gospel. "Yet I am not ashamed; for I know Him whom I have believed, and I am persuaded that He is able to guard that which I have committed unto Him against that day" (II. i. 12). Here, as elsewhere, the whole enjoyment of the gospel is made to turn on personal faith. The salvation of the gospel is universal, yet conditional; it avails for all, but those alone shall be saved who by faith accept it. Paul's faith had brought him into living connection with Jesus Christ, with Him he lived in daily communion, to Him he had committed all his interests. And he had the most confident persuasion that the Saviour would not fail him, even when no man stood by him.

The outlook for this world was very dark, the followers of Christ were being subjected to cruel persecution, but none of these things moved Paul the aged. He had put his life, his soul, his happiness, and his ministry into the hands of Jesus Christ, and he was confident that He would guard all until the day, now near at hand, when He would summon him into His presence to receive it back, and to enter for ever upon the joy of his Lord.

X

THE GOSPEL IN THE EPISTLE TO TITUS

ALMOST all that has been said regarding the genuineness of the Epistles to Timothy may be said of this letter to Titus: it is so evidently written by the same hand as penned the former. The subjects treated are the same, the mode in which the salvation of the gospel is presented is the same, many of the expressions are the same, and if we can trace the mind and pen of the great Apostle in the Epistles to Timothy, we cannot fail to note them in this letter.

It is addressed to Titus, whom Paul calls "his true child after a common faith" (i. 4), a name he might well apply to one of his earliest converts and most devoted fellow-labourers. From the first missionary journey almost to the close of his life, Titus was closely associated with Paul. After the departure of Barnabas he became his trusted companion, employed on several important and delicate missions. He was one of those friends who gathered round the Apostle after his first imprisonment, and accompanied him when he went forth once more to extend the Church of Christ, or to revisit some of the Churches in which he had always taken the deepest interest. Among the places they visited together was the Island of Crete, which has always had a bad reputation for the lawlessness of its inhabitants. Once before Paul had touched at this beautiful island on his memorable voyage to Rome, but it is not likely that he had any opportunity of preaching the gospel in Crete. As, however, it lay within easy reach of Asia Minor, Paul felt called upon to carry the gospel to its inhabitants. Finding it impossible to overtake the work there in the short time at his disposal, he left Titus behind to organise the small Church he had founded, and to instruct its members more fully in Christian faith. His presence was much needed. Ignorant and unstable as some of the Cretan converts were, they were susceptible of every passing influence. Judaising teachers appeared among them seeking to beguile them from the teaching of Paul; their minds were filled with silly fables instead of with the practical teaching of the Apostle. All this Paul learned through a communication from Titus, and he at once sent to his trusted fellow-labourer a letter in which he insisted on appointing to the oversight of these Churches men of approved Christian character who would be able to control the somewhat unruly members. Equally important was it that Titus should adhere to the sound teaching he had himself received. He was to keep before the minds of the Cretans the gospel as it had been delivered to himself. The gospel he was to preach was the gospel of a free and universal salvation, not, however, to be severed from holiness and purity of life in which some of the members of this Church were so deficient. We recognise the teaching as that of the other Epistles. "Which of all the Fathers of the first or second century was in the smallest degree capable of writing so masterly a formula of Christian doctrine and practice as these verses (ii. 11–14), or the perfectly independent, yet no less memorable, presentation of gospel truth—with a completeness only too many-sided for sects and parties —in iii. 5–7." [1]

A favourite expression in this Epistle is "God our Saviour" (i. 3, ii. 10, iii. 4). The superstitious pagan was afraid of his gods. His worship was founded on fear. He dreaded the unseen powers that dwelt in trees and streams, in mountains and valleys, and he was always trying to propitiate them. But Paul was able to speak of God as a Saviour whose love for the sinful race had led Him to send His Son to earth to work out the salvation He wished to offer to them. It is an echo of the Old Testament teaching with which the Apostle was familiar: "Look unto Me, and be ye saved, all the ends of the earth: for I am God, and there is none else" (Isa. xlv. 22).

Salvation, according to the writer of this letter, has its rise in God Himself. This is the view of it taken both by Jesus and by Paul. It is

[1] Farrar, *St. Paul*, ii. p. 536, note 2.

a travesty of the New Testament view of the work of Christ to represent it, as a certain school of fiction does, as teaching that God in His anger determined to destroy the human race, but that Jesus Christ by His sacrifice and death turned away His anger and made Him well disposed to poor sinners. The New Testament always traces salvation to the love of God. So Jesus has taught us in that wonderful saying which contains His gospel in one short sentence, "God so loved the world, that He gave His only begotten Son, that whosoever believeth on Him should not perish, but have eternal life" (John iii. 16). So Paul taught in the Epistle to the Romans: "God commendeth His own love toward us, in that, while we were yet sinners, Christ died for us" (Rom. v. 8). It is the same truth He affirms in this Epistle: "For the grace of God hath appeared, bringing salvation to all men" (Tit. ii. 11). "When the kindness of God our Saviour, and His love toward man, appeared" (Tit. iii. 4). The river has its birth in the melting of the snows under the sun's influence. Salvation flows from the heart of God, who has no pleasure in the death of the sinner. God is a just God and at the same time a Saviour, to whom the world owes the plan of salvation wrought out in the mission of Jesus Christ; for the word translated "appeared" is that which is generally applied to the manifestation of Christ on earth or in glory. The history of salvation is the history of divine grace in relation to a fallen race.

And salvation is of grace, not of human merit,

as we have also seen in the Epistle to the Ephesians. It is "not by works done in righteousness, which we did ourselves, but according to His mercy He saved us" (Tit. iii. 5). For the first effort of the awakened sinner is to save himself. His first question when he comes to know his sin and to realise his condemnation is "What shall I do?" It was the question asked by those who waited on the Baptist's ministry, and those whose consciences were pricked on the day of Pentecost. And we recognise in these words the echo of Paul's own experience. No man had laboured more earnestly than he had to establish a righteousness of his own, but the more earnest he became the more was he sensible of failure, and the more shut up to the mercy of God.

The experience of Augustine and Luther found expression in their strong denunciation of works as a condition of salvation, and in the manner in which they magnified the grace of God.

In the important passage (Tit. ii. 11–16) we have the central truth of Paul's gospel, that salvation is wrought out for us by Jesus Christ in His sacrifice and death. "He gave Himself for us, that He might redeem us from all iniquity" (ii. 14). The expression "gave Himself for us" is a favourite Pauline phrase for the death of Christ as the sinner's representative, and the preposition translated "for" though primarily expressing the thought, for the advantage of, carries with it in many passages the thought, instead of, and implies that Jesus took the sinner's place, and by so doing redeems him from all iniquity. He redeems him from the penalty in order to redeem him from the bondage. The one must precede the other, for no one can be freed from the dominion of sin who is left uncertain of his deliverance from the penalty which his past transgression has incurred. We recognise in this the characteristic Pauline gospel with which the other Epistles have made us familiar.

Here, too, we have the Pauline doctrine of justification, "that, being justified by His grace, we might be made heirs according to the hope of eternal life" (iii. 7). Though the grace of God brings this salvation to all men, it does not follow that all are saved. Those alone who accept this grace, those alone who believe on the Saviour, are justified, *i.e.* reckoned as having in Christ paid the penalty demanded by the law. It is faith which unites the sinner to Christ and thus makes Him partaker of His perfect righteousness. To use the words of the Shorter Catechism, which is perhaps the most concise exposition of this teaching: "Justification is an act of God's free grace, wherein He pardoneth all our sins, and accepteth us as righteous in His sight, only for the righteousness of Christ imputed to us and received by faith alone." Nor can the sinner claim any merit for his faith. If faith were the sole factor in this great change, he might take credit for his faith, and trace his salvation after all to his own works. But the Apostle reminds us here that faith itself is the work of God, the result of the effectual working of the Holy Spirit. "Not by works done in righteousness, but according to His mercy He saved us, through the washing of regeneration and the renewing of the Holy Ghost, which He poured out upon us richly, through Jesus Christ our Saviour" (iii. 5, 6). The heart is so deceitful, so desperately wicked, so hard and cold and dead, that it needs a divine power to quicken and warm, to soften and renew it. It is impossible to tell where the divine ends and the human begins. The sinner may not be able to explain how serious thought was awakened, but he has not been able to extinguish the divine spark, which has been fanned into a flame of loving trust in Jesus, who gave Himself for the sinner. Thus, in the mysterious operation of grace, the work of salvation is brought about in the most natural way. The sinner, arrested in his course, begins to think seriously, repents of his sin, grasps eagerly at the forgiveness offered him in the gospel, puts his trust in Jesus as the Saviour, and enters into peace. But behind this natural process there is a divine and invisible influence at work, without which the sinner would never have stopped to consider his ways. We are reminded by this passage of Paul's thought and language in the Epistles to the Romans and Galatians. When he speaks of one of the agencies of salvation as the "washing or laver of regeneration," it is, of course, open to question whether these words refer to baptism at all. It is quite possible to regard the expression as a mere figure to set forth the sanctifying influence of the Holy Spirit which is essential to the salvation of the sinner. We are reminded of the Saviour's own words, "Except a man be born of water and the Spirit, he cannot enter into the kingdom of God" (John iii. 5). If the reference be to baptism, the idea of baptismal regeneration is excluded both by the words that precede and follow the expression. The meaning is well brought out by Godet when he says, "The pardon which is represented by water baptism is only the negative condition, the *sine qua non* of the new birth. The positive principle of this inner fact is the Spirit whom God gives to the soul which has been washed from its sin."[1]

It was important, too, that Titus in his teaching of the Cretan Church should insist that the gospel salvation was a salvation from sin, and required the saved sinner to follow after holiness. "The grace of God hath appeared, bringing salvation to all men, instructing us, to the intent that, denying ungodliness and worldly lusts, we should live soberly and righteously and godly in this present world" (Tit. ii. 12). "Christ gave Himself for us, that He might redeem us from all iniquity, and purify unto Himself a people for His own possession, zealous of good works" (ii. 14). "Faithful is the saying, and concerning these things I will that thou affirm confidently, to the end that they which have believed God may be careful to maintain good works" (iii. 8). How necessary such teaching was in Crete appears from the first chapter of this Epistle, in which the character of the

---

[1] Godet, *Gospel of John*, iii. 5. See also Ellicott on the *Pastoral Epistles*, Titus iii. 5.

8

islanders is described. Surrounded, too, as the converts were by their old companions and temptations, the utmost vigilance was required on their part lest they should be again overcome by their old habits. The Christian, instead of being less careful of himself, is bound to be more careful. The law still remains a rule of life, and instead of relaxing their obedience, they were required to be more zealous in maintaining it. They were to deny themselves, not only an ungodly manner of living, but all inordinate desire for the things of this world. As those who were risen with Christ, they were to seek the things that are above, and not the things that are upon the earth; and they were to cultivate a sober, righteous, and godly life. For the cultivation of such a life no motive could be stronger than the speedy return of Jesus Christ to this earth. "Looking for the blessed hope and appearing of the glory of our great God and Saviour Jesus Christ" (ii. 13). The same argument was used with the Philippians, who were exhorted to a holy life by the consideration that they were "looking for a Saviour, the Lord Jesus Christ." For Jesus was to complete the salvation of His people by appearing again in glory. This, too, was part of Paul's gospel, following the teaching of our Lord Himself. This state of trouble in which the believer finds himself is not to last for ever. Evil is not always to triumph. The Christians were not to be always exposed to persecution and suffering in the cause of Christ. Jesus was to appear again, not in the garments of poverty, despised and rejected by men, but in the glory of the Father, rejoicing the hearts of all those who loved Him and were looking for His appearing.

This appearing of Christ in glory is generally associated with His coming to judge the world in righteousness. If the Cretan converts kept this truth before them, it was impossible they could yield to worldly lusts. They were to give account of themselves to Christ at His appearing in glory. For He who came into the world and lived as a man among men, He who gave His life for men that He might redeem them from all iniquity, is one day to be manifested in glory, and to obtain recognition from His redeemed people as the great Lord and Saviour, unto whom with the Father we ascribe all glory and dominion for ever and ever.

XI

THE GOSPEL IN THE EPISTLE TO THE HEBREWS

THE Epistles we have passed under review are those more or less accepted as the writings of the Apostle Paul. We have been able to gather from them what was the great Apostle's conception of the gospel. We turn now to an Epistle which occupies a different position in the New Testament. Its heading in our Bibles is "Epistle of Paul the Apostle to the Hebrews." But in the older MSS. it is simply "to the Hebrews." There is nothing, however, in the letter itself to indicate by whom it was written, or to what particular Church it was sent. It was long accepted as the work of the Apostle Paul, but scarcely any critic of repute now holds that view. It has been variously ascribed to Luke, to Apollos, to Barnabas, to Silas, and to Clement of Rome. Some regard it as proceeding from one who was imbued with the spirit and teaching of Paul, or who formed one of the inner circle of his friends; others as emanating from one whose view of

Christ and His gospel was entirely different from that of Paul. It may suffice to say that the balance of opinion in our day is divided between Apollos and Barnabas, although one writer has been at great pains to indicate the points of resemblance between the language of the Hebrews and that of the Acts of the Apostles and the Pastoral Epistles.[1] It is not necessary to decide on a question so much disputed. The important point is, that we have in this Epistle a view of the gospel entertained in the first century of the Church, which we shall find to be on all essential points the same as that presented by the Apostle Paul. The writer may differ in his point of view, and also in his line of thought. He may view the priesthood of Christ as carried on in the heavenly sanctuary, as Dr. Bruce insists, whereas Paul centres our attention on the Cross, but he too recognises that the removal of sin is due to the one offering of Himself made by Jesus.

We find the same difference of opinion regarding the persons designated the Hebrews, to whom the letter was addressed. Were they the Hebrew Christians generally, or were they connected with one particular Church, and if so, with what Church? Here, again, we do not get much light from the letter itself. It does not bear on the face of it that it is addressed to any particular Church. It has no introduction, but plunges at once *in medias res.* The Churches of Rome, Alexandria, Antioch in Syria, and Jerusalem have

[1] The Rev. W. H. Simcox in *The Expositor,* 1888.

been suggested, but there is no general agreement on the subject. All are agreed that it was addressed to some little community of Jewish Christians, who were thoroughly acquainted with the history of their nation and also with the elaborate ceremonialism of Jewish worship. In consequence of the persecution to which they had been exposed, and the little progress they had made in Christian knowledge, these Hebrew Christians were in danger of drifting away from the faith they had embraced. They were so filled with the old prejudices of their nation that they stumbled at several things in Christianity. Professor Bruce in his writings on this Epistle sums these up under three points: 1st, the superseding of an ancient divinely-appointed religion by what appeared to be a novelty and an innovation; 2nd, the humiliation and sufferings of Jesus regarded as the Christ; 3rd, the absence from Christianity of a priesthood and a sacrificial ritual.[1] The burden of the letter is to demonstrate the infinite superiority of the Christian dispensation to that of Judaism. This is done by exhibiting the divine dignity of its Author, the honour attaching to His priesthood as evidenced by its antiquity, its permanence, and the all-sufficient and eternal value of His atoning sacrifice. It is when we come to consider this last point that we find the writer teaching the same gospel as is contained in the Pauline Epistles—the same gospel preached by Jesus and His apostles. Nor is the argument for

[1] Bruce, *Epistle to the Hebrews*, Introduction.

the superiority of the Christian dispensation a new one. It is certainly implied in the Epistles to the Romans, II. Corinthians, and Galatians. The more carefully we study the contents of the Epistle the more does it become apparent that the unknown author of this interesting and most elaborate letter is at one with the great Apostle in his views as to the person and work of Jesus Christ.

The author of the Epistle to the Hebrews has a most exalted conception of the person of Christ. Jesus Christ is not only the last, He is by far the most glorious messenger by whom God has made known His will to men. The Jews could boast of a long and honourable roll of prophets by whom God had revealed Himself to their fathers, men who saw visions of the Almighty, who had been in His secret place, who had heard His voice in their inmost souls, and had felt constrained to deliver His message to their fellow-men. But Jesus was the Son of God. The Jew might further boast that the law had been given by angels, and that these bright spirits played an important part in the nation's history; but no angel could claim the glory and honour belonging to Jesus Christ. In the first two chapters the writer demonstrates the superiority of Jesus to the angels. He is the eternal Son of God, the occupant of His throne for ever and ever, receiving the same worship in heaven as the Almighty Father. By Him all things were created. He is the effulgence of the Father's glory, and the very image of His substance. Besides this honour which Jesus derived from the past, the writer dwells with fond satisfaction on that to which He had been now exalted. For as the reward of His deep humiliation, He has been raised to the head of the new creation, exercising dominion over the universe of God, thus in His own person raising the once sinful race of man to a position of superiority over the angels of God. We recognise this view of Christ as one with which the Pauline Epistles have made us familiar.[1]

This divine glory of Jesus was not, however, in the writer's opinion, inconsistent with His humanity. Jesus did not merely assume the appearance of man, as some have interpreted the words in Phil. ii. 7; He partook of flesh and blood, and was made of the seed of Abraham (Heb. ii. 14–16), bone of our bone and flesh of our flesh. "He was made like unto His brethren," passed through the whole round of human experience, "He suffered being tempted," and so can enter with the most intense sympathy into the life of every sinner who comes to Him. The human side of the Saviour is very dear to the writer of this Epistle; for he feels that the troubled heart of man wants a human friend to whom to unburden itself. Romanism and Ritualism offer that friend in the priest of the confessional, but Christianity offers Jesus Himself, the Friend of sinners. Putting together the two aspects, the divine and the human in Jesus Christ, the writer thus encourages the Hebrew

[1] Col. i. 15-18; Phil. ii. 6-11.

Christians: "Having then a great high priest, who is passed into the heavens, Jesus the Son of God, let us hold fast our confession. For we have not an high priest that cannot be touched with a feeling of our infirmities; but one that hath been in all points tempted like as we are, yet without sin."[1]

No names were more honoured by the Jews than those of Moses and Aaron. The former was the great leader and lawgiver of God's ancient people. Yet Moses was far inferior to Jesus Christ, the Captain of salvation, the Messenger of the new covenant. He was the servant of God; Jesus was His Son. He promised rest to the wearied host he led through the wilderness, but he was not able to bring them into it. Jesus gives rest now and here, for the soul that accepts and trusts Him enters into rest. The latter, Aaron, was called of God to be the high priest of his nation, through whom the people might draw nigh to God. For many years he held that honourable office, handing it down on his death to his descendants, who had ever since continued to discharge it. The Christian religion apparently had no priest, and so in the eyes of the Jews was much inferior to Judaism. The writer of this Epistle proceeds to remove this stumbling-block, and to show that Jesus far excelled in the honour and dignity of His priestly office even Aaron himself. The Aaronic priesthood dated only from the wilderness; Jesus belonged to a priesthood of a much older date and more exalted rank, that of

[1] Heb. iv. 14-16.

Melchizedek. The priesthood of Aaron and of all his successors was exercised only for the short period of their natural lives, and was constantly changing. Jesus, on the other hand, has an unchanging priesthood which death cannot affect. Aaron ministered in a frail tabernacle made with hands, and his successors, in after times, in the magnificent house erected by Solomon for the divine worship. And even in these sanctuaries it was only once a year that the high priest was permitted to enter into the presence of the divine symbol, and there to intercede for the nation and for himself. Jesus as the high priest of the new dispensation ministers in the spiritual temple, in the immediate presence of God Himself, where He ever dwells, and so makes continual intercession on behalf of His own people.

If the author of this letter dwells with pride on the person and high official standing of Jesus Christ compared with the most illustrious prophets, lawgivers, and priests of the Jews, he lays special stress on the infinite superiority of the sacrifice Jesus presented to God over all the offerings of the Jewish priests. Every morning and evening the priests presented their sacrifices and interceded for the people, but the sacrifice of to-day had no value for to-morrow. The worshipper came to the feasts and brought his offering and was assured of forgiveness, but he had to return next year and repeat his offering and have his pardon renewed. Thus it was borne home to the conscience of the Jew that these sacrifices could never take away sin. They only symbolised and pointed him forward to the one great sacrifice, to be offered up in the fulness of the time. But Jesus, a priest of more illustrious descent than any Jewish priest, honoured by Heaven as none of them had ever been, has "a sacrifice of richer blood and nobler name" to present to His Father. He is Himself both priest and sacrifice, for the offering He has to present is nothing less than His own body. "Now once at the end of the ages hath He been manifested to put away sin by the sacrifice of Himself" (Heb. ix. 26). "He, when He had offered one sacrifice for sins for ever, sat down on the right hand of God" (Heb. x. 12). "Christ also was once offered to bear the sins of many" (Heb. ix. 28). "He made propitiation for the sins of the people" (Heb. ii. 17). A sacrifice like that did not need to be repeated, and could not be repeated. By it the sin of the world has been taken away, and an atonement has been made for all who chose to avail themselves of it. The way has been opened up into the immediate presence of God. "Christianity is the perfect and final religion because it brings man nigh to God."[1] It is true the worshipper is ever committing sin, but he needs no new sacrifice for his sins. He falls back on the sacrifice once offered, on the ground of which he has the assurance of God in the new covenant: "I will be merciful to their iniquities, and their sins will I remember no more" (Heb. viii. 12). The blood shed on Calvary will

[1] Bruce, *Epistle to the Hebrews*, Introduction.

never be shed again. Its voice is never silent, it speaks better things than that of Abel. With that blood in His hands the Saviour has passed into the true sanctuary, where He ever liveth to make intercession, and it is impossible to imagine that intercession failing in its purpose. Nor will the virtue of His sacrifice ever be exhausted. The worshippers may pass from the courts below to the heavenly sanctuary, others may take their places, but for them too this great sacrifice avails, "He hath offered one sacrifice for sins for ever."

One grim fact remains apparently unaffected by all the sacrifices of the priests or even by the sacrifice of Christ, and that is death. The physical penalty of the broken law remains. Even the sacrifice of Christ has not removed this; death has still dominion over man. That is so far true, but it is only a partial truth. It is true Jesus died, but unlike the Jewish priests He did not see corruption. "He tasted death for every man." But in the great conflict in which He too became the tenant of the grave He secured the victory for the race; for when He rose from the dead "He destroyed him that had the power of death, that is, the devil; and delivered them who through fear of death were all their lifetime subject to bondage" (Heb. ii. 14, 15). For what is the power of death but the terror of the unknown? What is it but the fear lest our misdeeds here shall be visited in the future? But Jesus has removed this fear. He has made propitiation for sin, and His risen life is the pledge that all who believe in Him shall share with Him the glories and the joys of His exalted state. For as the writer of this letter contemplates Jesus he sees "Him who hath been made a little lower than the angels, even Jesus, because of the suffering of death crowned with glory and honour" (Heb. ii. 9). He sees Him bringing many sons to glory, and sitting down on the right hand of God in the peaceful enjoyment of His triumph.

Such is the gospel in the Epistle to the Hebrews. It matters little who the author was. He was one who firmly believed the good tidings that Jesus Christ came into the world to save sinners. He believed that He died for the ungodly, that He made propitiation for iniquity, and that by His sacrifice He took away sin. He believed in His resurrection and exaltation, and in His ever present sympathy with His Church and people. He teaches the same truth as Paul taught. He knows no other gospel than Jesus Christ and Him crucified.

XII

THE GOSPEL IN THE EPISTLES OF PETER

IF we possess in the Epistle to the Hebrews a view of Christianity as it appeared to minds more or less influenced by the teaching of the Apostle Paul, we have in these letters a conception of the gospel formed by one who was a close friend of the Founder of Christianity, and had been associated with Jesus during His public ministry. Peter was one of the first who obeyed the summons of Jesus of Nazareth to follow Him, and formed one of the inner circle of the disciples who were especially favoured by their Master. He had thus peculiar advantages for hearing the teaching of the Saviour. He had visions of His glory in the house of Jairus and on the Mount of Transfiguration; he had a glimpse into the depth of His humiliation in the garden of Gethsemane, and these events made a lasting impression on his mind. Dean Farrar says, "We have in verse after verse the indications of subtle reminiscences, such as must have lingered in the mind of St. Peter."[1] From the first he had formed

[1] *Early Days of Christianity*, i. p. 124.

an exalted conception of Jesus of Nazareth. The fame of His mighty works and His wonderful teaching was ringing through the land, and each man was asking his neighbour, "What manner of man is this?" Is he a prophet? Whence has He obtained His wisdom? Peter affirmed: "Thou art the Christ, the Son of the living God" (Matt. xvi. 16). Few therefore had so many opportunities for observing the main drift of the Saviour's teaching regarding His own mission to this world. He was present, most likely, at the interview with Nicodemus. The invitation, "Come unto Me, all ye that labour and are heavy laden," was uttered in his hearing. He must have heard His kind words to the woman that was a sinner and to Zacchæus the publican. He would remember the remarkable saying with which He rebuked the unseemly strife that had arisen among the disciples: "The Son of man came not to be ministered unto, but to minister, and give His life a ransom for many" (Matt. xx. 28), as well as the words in which He explained to the inquiring Greeks the reasonableness of His death. Often, too, had Jesus, especially during His last days with them, spoken of His approaching sufferings and death and resurrection. These talks he could never forget, for had not the withering rebuke of Jesus impressed them indelibly on memory when Peter ventured to remonstrate with Him for mentioning such subjects? Little as he understood these words at the time, the resurrection and ascension, and, above all, the descent of the Spirit at Pentecost, gave them a new life and meaning. The discourses preserved in the Acts of the Apostles show us what a clear conception he had of the Saviour's person and work. There we find the germ of his teaching in these Epistles. He presented Jesus to his countrymen as the eternal Son of God who had been ordained to be the Saviour of the world, and in accordance with that appointment came into the world, and after a life spent in doing good had been cruelly put to death.

His death, divinely arranged and voluntarily submitted to, was necessary to secure the salvation of man. From death Jesus had been raised by God the Father, exalted to His own right hand, made a Prince and a Saviour to give repentance and the remission of sins (Acts iii. 13–15, v. 30, 31). The aim of His mission was to bless men in turning every one of them from their iniquities. Salvation was to be found in Him alone; "for neither is there any other name under heaven, that is given among men, wherein we must be saved" (Acts iv. 12).

Peter, too, was chosen to open the door of the Christian Church to the Gentiles, and was thus brought into contact with the great Apostle of the Gentiles, to whose mission he gave the stamp of his approval. And one cannot fail to notice the harmony there is between the writings of Peter and the Epistles of Paul on the subject of the gospel. For the whole effort of the Tübingen School has been to divorce the teaching of Paul from that of the other Apostles. The theory is made to turn on the memorable quarrel between the two men recorded in Gal. ii. 11–13. But neither in the Acts of the Apostles nor in the Epistles is there any proof of this divorce. On the contrary, it has been pointed out by critics of different schools that there is a common likeness between the teaching of both Apostles. Thus Wiesinger says, "Peter in his Epistle to the Pauline Churches has impressed the seal of his testimony on the gospel as preached by Paul."[1] Huther remarks that "the Christianity of Peter is the same as that of Paul and John."[2] And Weiss comes to the conclusion that "Peter wished by his apostolic testimony to confirm the teaching already delivered to his readers."[3] It is essentially the same gospel the two men teach. With both the death of Christ is the central point of the whole work of redemption, only the method of stating it differs with the mental constitution and the standpoint of either writer. The one is more didactic in his mode of presenting the truth, the other more practical.

After his temporary estrangement from Paul the movements of Peter are really unknown to us. We can only surmise from the salutation of his First Epistle that he may have visited the Churches in Asia Minor founded by Paul. It is a very generally accepted tradition that he visited Rome during the last year of Paul's life, and suffered martyrdom

---

[1] Meyer's *Commentary I. Peter*, Eng. trans. p. 12.
[2] *Ibid.*   [3] *Ibid.*

in that city shortly after the Apostle of the Gentiles. From Rome he was believed to have written the letters that bear his name.

The genuineness of the First Epistle is generally accepted. "The First Epistle is one of the writings of the New Testament which are the most anciently and most unanimously quoted as authentic."[1] It is the very reverse with the Second, which, however Petrine in thought, is not now regarded as the work of the Apostle, though bearing the impress of his influence, and undoubtedly dating from Apostolic times.

The First Epistle is addressed to "the sojourners of the Dispersion in Pontus, Galatia, Cappadocia, Asia, and Bithynia" (I. i. 1), very largely therefore to the members of the Churches founded by the Apostle Paul. From the fact that Peter associates with himself Silvanus and Mark, both of whom had been companions of Paul at Rome, it has been thought that the letter was written after the death of the Apostle of the Gentiles. These sojourners whom he addressed were not novices in the Christian life. They had made considerable advances in knowledge and experience, but had entered on a time of trial which was testing the reality of their faith, was separating the gold from the dross, and was strengthening those ties of brotherly kindness which bind Christians so closely to one another. And so the Apostle writes his letter to encourage them to patience and endurance by the example of Jesus Christ and the great hope laid up for

[1] Renan, *Antichrist*, Eng. trans. Introduction, p. vii.

them in the gospel, and also to holiness of life as a sure means of influencing their heathen neighbours.

These letters are full of subtle touches that remind one of the teaching of Jesus, and of the personal life of Jesus, with which the writer was so familiar. In the first chapter he speaks of God as the Father, a favourite expression of the Saviour's. The salvation which has come to man through Christ is specially referred to as the subject of Old Testament prophecy. The Jewish rabbis had always recognised the prophecies referring to the glories of Messiah; it was left to Jesus to open the understandings of His disciples as He "said unto them, Thus it is written, that the Christ should suffer, and rise again from the dead the third day; and that repentance and remission of sins should be preached in His name unto all nations" (Luke xxiv. 46). And Peter, writing of salvation, says, "concerning which salvation the prophets sought and searched diligently, who prophesied of the grace that should come unto you: searching what time, or what manner of time the Spirit of Christ which was in them did point unto, when it testified beforehand the sufferings of Christ, and the glories that should follow them" (I. i. 10, 11). Whatever view we take of the authorship of the Second Epistle we cannot fail to recognise two personal reminiscences of Peter's. He reminds those to whom he was writing, "that the putting off of my tabernacle cometh swiftly, even as our Lord Jesus Christ signified to me" (II. i. 14; comp. with

John xxi. 18). And referring to the importance of his teaching, he remarks, "We did not follow cunningly devised fables, when we made known unto you the power and coming of our Lord Jesus Christ, but we were eye-witnesses of His majesty. For He received from God the Father honour and glory, when there came such a voice to Him from the excellent glory, This is My beloved Son, in whom I am well pleased: and this voice we ourselves heard come out of heaven, when we were with Him in the holy mount" (II. i. 16–18).

With reference to the death of Christ, the teaching of Peter in these letters shows that it was the same gospel he had proclaimed in the Churches of Asia Minor as Paul himself had preached. It is quite true the death of Christ is alluded to chiefly as an example of the sublime patience of Jesus under suffering, and with reference to its moral effects on the believer, as Pfleiderer very correctly points out;[1] but the language plainly implies a previous reconciliation from guilt; the language is so precise, the expressions are so definite, that it is scarcely possible to doubt that Peter, like Paul, traces the salvation of man to the death of Jesus Christ. What other construction can be put on the opening verses of the Epistle, where he addresses the sojourners in the Churches as "elect . . . according to the foreknowledge of God the Father, in sanctification of the Spirit, unto obedience and sprinkling of the blood of Christ" (I. i. 2)? And although he speaks

[1] Pfleiderer's *Paulinismus*, Eng. trans. ii. p. 150.

of their redemption as delivering them from their vain manner of life, it surely cannot be said that this excludes their state of condemnation, especially when it is purchased by the blood of Christ, and connected in thought with the Paschal Lamb: "Knowing that ye were redeemed, not with corruptible things, with silver and gold, from your vain manner of life handed down from your fathers; but with precious blood, as of a lamb without blemish and without spot, even the blood of Christ" (I. i. 18, 19). It is the same teaching that runs through the Pauline Epistles: "Redemption through His blood, the forgiveness of our trespasses" (Eph. i. 7), although Peter is thinking more of the practical results that flow from the redemptive work of Christ. Again, when he recommends them to be patient under the ill-treatment of their enemies, he reminds them of the example of the suffering Christ; but he sets Him before them as having suffered for their sins. It was this consideration that was fitted to move them to follow in the footsteps of the meek and patient Sufferer: "Christ also suffered for you"—and the meaning is not altered whether you read it "on your behalf" or "in your stead"—"an example, that ye should follow His steps; who did no sin, neither was guile found in His mouth; who, when He was reviled, reviled not again; when He suffered, threatened not; but committed Himself to Him that judgeth righteously: who His own self bare our sins in His body upon the tree, that we, having died unto sins, might live unto righteousness; by whose stripes ye were healed" (I. ii. 21–24). Not till in Christ they had died to sin was it possible for them to live this new life of likeness to Christ.

Here, again, we are on familiar ground. We have found this in Paul's gospel: "Him who knew no sin He made to be sin on our behalf; that we might become the righteousness of God in Him" (II. Cor. v. 21). Both Peter and Paul had learned the truth from the same Master, and been enlightened by the same Spirit. They were not the leaders of rival schools. They both gloried in the Cross of Christ. The same argument is repeated in the next chapter. Conscious of their innocence of the charges brought against them by their pagan neighbours, and of the injustice of the persecutions they endured, the Christians might become restless, and might even retaliate on their enemies. Such conduct would be unbecoming the followers of Jesus Christ, who "also suffered for sins once, the righteous for the unrighteous, that He might bring us to God; being put to death in the flesh, but quickened in the spirit" (I. iii. 18). Here again the purpose of Christ's death is stated almost in Pauline terms to be to bring us to God, a thought that is constantly finding expression in the Epistles to the Corinthians, Romans, and Ephesians. For the far off must first be brought near if they are henceforth to follow closely in the steps of Christ and be conformed to His image.

It is, however, on the risen and glorified Christ

that the Apostle Peter keeps his eye fixed. The resurrection and revelation of Jesus Christ are favourite topics in these Epistles, as fitted to supply the highest encouragement and hope to the persecuted Christians of the Dispersion. Their lot in this life might have very little to relieve the darkness and depression in which they lived. They might be called upon to suffer the loss of all things, and even to suffer the martyr's death; but there was a great hope which was fitted to fill them with joy unspeakable and full of glory: "Blessed be the God and Father of our Lord Jesus Christ, who according to His great mercy begat us again unto a living hope by the resurrection of Jesus Christ from the dead, unto an inheritance incorruptible, and undefiled, and that fadeth not away, reserved in heaven for you, who by the power of God are guarded unto salvation ready to be revealed in the last time" (I. i. 3–5).

I need scarcely say that in such a practical letter Peter insists on the moral effects of the gospel in producing holiness of heart and life. He calls upon the scattered Christians to be holy in all manner of living; to abstain from fleshly lusts which war against the soul, and to stand fast in the true grace of God; and he closes with the assurance which may be said to sum up all his teaching: "The God of all grace, who called you unto His eternal glory in Christ, after that ye have suffered a while, shall Himself perfect, stablish, strengthen you. To Him be the dominion for ever and ever. Amen" (I. v. 11).

XIII

THE GOSPEL IN THE EPISTLES OF JOHN

BRIEF comparison between these Epistles and the Fourth Gospel is sufficient to prove that they are from the pen of the same writer. The style is the same, the language is the same, the subject-matter is the same. Both, too, were evidently written about the same time. If, then, the author of the Fourth Gospel was the Apostle John, and we may take it that that is now the general opinion of the Church, then these Epistles too are from his pen. We recognise in them the same difference in viewing the person and work of Jesus as we find between the Fourth Gospel and the Synoptic Gospels. The three leading words in the gospel are life, light, love, and we find the writer dwelling on those words in the Epistles. And while the author of the Fourth Gospel tells us that it was written that men " might believe that Jesus is the Christ, the Son of God; and that believing they might have life in His name" (John xx. 31), the author of these letters assures us that he sought to declare to men " the life, the

eternal life, which was with the Father, and was manifested; that ye might have fellowship with us: yea, and our fellowship is with the Father, and with His Son Jesus Christ" (I. i. 2, 3). "These things have I written unto you, that ye may know that ye have eternal life, even unto you that believe on the name of the Son of God" (I. v. 13).

In attempting, then, to form a conception of the gospel presented in the Epistles of John, we have not only the advantage of having the views of one who was a close personal friend of Jesus, of one whose loving heart saw deeper into the inner life of Jesus than any of his companions, but of one who has already given us his impressions of the person, life, and sayings of Jesus. We can compare the Epistles with the Gospels, and if we find the view of Jesus given in both is the same, and if we find that this again is practically the same with the gospel Paul proclaimed, then we may conclude that in his Epistles Paul presented the gospel as it was held by the Apostles of Jesus and received in the Church. We know that the Apostle John was in closer touch with Jesus than any of his brother disciples. He was known as the "disciple whom Jesus loved." His contemplative mind was constantly dwelling on the person of Jesus and on His utterances, and we feel at once that he knew the mind of his Master better than any of his contemporaries. It is not unlikely that we have in his gospel the essence of his own teaching when he was exhorting the

Churches, and we may take it for granted that it was written at some time in his ministry when he had leisure to mature the fruit of his lifelong contemplation. This leisure was found during the period of his banishment to Patmos "for the word of God and the testimony of Jesus." His Epistles appear to have been written about the same time. The Second and Third are addressed to two friends. The First has nothing to indicate to whom it was addressed. It has the appearance of being a kind of summary of his teaching, and may have been sent along with his Gospel when it was forwarded to the Churches, as explaining the reasons that had led the Apostle to give to the world his reminiscences of Jesus. It is a kind of prefatory letter in which the writer states that his conception of Jesus and His work was the result of personal observation and experience, unlike that of the Evangelist Luke, who tells us that his facts were gathered from the best sources open to him. The First Epistle gives us the same sublime conception of Jesus as we find in the Fourth Gospel. One can scarcely fail to notice the close connection there is between the prologue of the Gospel and the first words of this Epistle: "Jesus is the Word of Life which was from the beginning, the eternal life which was with the Father" (I. i. 1, 2), and these expressions are characteristic of the Fourth Gospel. John was the first to apply the title of "The Word" to Jesus. It is true the term was in use among some of the speculative minds of his day, but he alone was bold enough to apply it to the relation in which Jesus stood to God. The human mind cannot form any conception of God. He is pure spirit, filling all space, dwelling in light to which no man can approach, whom "no man hath seen at any time." Spirit has neither form nor voice. But the Son of God was the perfect expression of the mind of the Eternal Spirit. His thought found utterance in His Son, His will was expressed by the acts of His Son, He was seen in the person of His Son. How John came to form this conception of the man Jesus it is impossible to say. He was in advance of all the men of his time. Peter, indeed, had once declared that Jesus was "the Christ, the Son of the living God" (Matt. xvi. 16); but he was far from rising to such a conception of Jesus as John had formed. He saw the divine glory shining around Him, he recognised in Him the Messiah of his nation, but it is questionable if Peter ever thought of Him as God manifest in the flesh. To John, the Man of Sorrows, who bore the reproach of His fellow-men, who was so misrepresented and misunderstood, and who ended His life on the Cross, on whose bosom he used to lean, was no other than God Himself who had been pleased to take a human form in the interest of man. Joseph and Mary wondered at the name given to their child, "Immanuel, God with us," but Mary never seemed to grasp what her Son meant by calling God His Father. To John it was the only explanation of His life; the sayings and doings of the man Jesus were the words and works of God Himself.

This high conception of Jesus did not, however, prevent John from recognising His true human nature. Already some were teaching in the Church that Jesus was not a real man, or rather, I should say, that the Christ was not a real man. Some held that during the public ministry of Jesus the spirit of the Christ had dwelt in Him and left Him at His death. Others thought of Him only as a phantom, the creature of the disciples' imagination, present only with them in their contemplative moods. They did not believe in the historic Christ. To John the Word of Life was a man of flesh and blood, whom he had seen with his eyes, whom he had handled with his hands, with whom he had walked up and down, whose words he had heard with his ears. He had seen Him faint and hungry after a long journey, or asleep after His hard labour. He had seen Him shedding the tears of sorrow. He had seen Him bowed in agony in the garden. He had seen the cruel nails driven through His hands and feet, and His dead body laid in the tomb. "That which was from the beginning, that which we have heard, that which we have seen with our eyes and our hands have handled of the Word of life . . . declare we unto you" (I. i. 1, 2). John insists on this all through these Epistles, because of the false teachers who were spreading their views. "Every spirit which confesseth that Jesus Christ is come in the flesh is of God; and every spirit which confesseth not Jesus is not of God" (I. iv. 3). "This is He that came by water and blood, even Jesus Christ" (I. v. 6). "Many deceivers are gone forth into the world, even they that confess not that Jesus Christ cometh in the flesh" (II. 7).

For what purpose, then, had the Son of God appeared as the man Christ Jesus? For what purpose was "the Word made flesh"? Was it that men might believe in the existence of the one living and true God? Was it that they might come to understand the deepest problems of existence through the revelations Jesus had made to them? That was one purpose, but it was not the main end of the incarnation. In the Fourth Gospel Jesus is represented as telling Nicodemus that "God gave His only begotten Son, that whosoever believeth on Him should not perish, but have eternal life" (John iii. 16). On another occasion He told His disciples, "I, if I be lifted up from the earth, will draw all men unto Myself" (John xii. 32). In this Epistle he is no less explicit in the reason he assigns for the divine manifestation in Jesus Christ. "And ye know that He was manifested to take away sins" (I. iii. 5). "To this end was the Son of God manifested, that He might destroy the works of the devil" (I. iii. 8). . John, like his Master, saw that this world had passed under the dominion of Satan, whom Jesus called "the prince of this world," but he saw further that the advent of the Son of God was in order to overthrow this dominion and establish the kingdom of God once more on earth.

Again, John gives us a view of the purpose of the Son of God's mission to this world, with which Jesus Himself has made us familiar, and which is frequently set forth in the Pauline Epistles, "We have beheld and bear witness that the Father hath sent the Son to be the Saviour of the world" (I. iv. 14). This is the truth we find in the Gospels: "Thou shalt call His name Jesus; for it is He that shall save His people from their sins" (Matt. i. 21). "The Son of Man came to seek and to save that which was lost" (Luke xix. 10). This is Paul's explanation of the incarnation: "Christ Jesus came into the world to save sinners, of whom I am chief" (I. Tim. i. 15). And John is quite as emphatic as the Saviour Himself or as the Apostle Paul as to the means by which Jesus was to effect this work of salvation: "He is the propitiation for our sins; and not for ours only, but also for the whole world" (II. ii. 2). "Herein was the love of God manifested in us, that God hath sent His only begotten Son into the world, that we might live through Him. Herein is love, not that we loved God, but that He loved us, and sent His Son to be the propitiation for our sins" (I. iv. 9, 10). The salvation of fallen man is thus traced to the love of God the Father, who made the greatest possible sacrifice He could make by giving up His own Son. And yet though Jesus was the gift of the Father's love, He was to accomplish the salvation of the world by becoming the propitiation for its sins. For great as the Father's love for sinners was, there was something standing in the way of His extending pardon, someone who needed to be propitiated. The word propitiation, though differing slightly from that used by Paul in the passage in which he teaches the same truth (Rom. iii. 25), is akin to it, and can best be understood by the word propitiatory sacrifice. " It is a sacrificial metaphor. . . . The word stands in close relation to the word mercy-seat, which—sprinkled with the blood of atonement, and dimly seen in the darkness through the clouds of incense—was a type of the means whereby man may stand redeemed and accepted in the presence of God."[1] In another passage the forgiveness of sins is said to be effected by the blood of Christ, as if John had present to his mind the words of Jesus at the Supper Table, " This is My blood of the covenant, which is shed for many unto remission of sins " (Matt. xxvi. 28); " The blood of Jesus His Son cleanseth us from all sin " (I. i. 7), where the death of Christ is regarded as the ground both of the justification and complete sanctification of the individual. The work of Christ is thus viewed in this Epistle as coextensive with human sin. If the propitiation is for the sins of the whole world, then condemnation must fall on all who do not put their faith in this divine propitiation made for and offered to them. " He that believeth not hath been judged already, because he hath not believed on the name of the only begotten Son of God "(John iii. 18).

In his Epistles John lays great stress on the necessity of faith on the part of the individual

[1] Farrar, *Early Days of Christianity*, ii. p. 411.

in order to his participation in the salvation of Jesus Christ. We have seen how he does so in his Gospel: "Whosoever believeth on Him shall not perish, but have eternal life" (John iii. 16). "This is the work of God, that ye believe on Him whom He hath sent" (John vi. 29).

Here he is quite as emphatic. "This is His commandment, that we should believe in the name of His Son Jesus Christ" (I. iii. 23). "He that believeth on the Son of God hath the witness in him: he that believeth not God hath made Him a liar; because he hath not believed in the witness that God hath borne concerning His Son. And the witness is this, that God gave unto us eternal life, and this life is in His Son. He that hath the Son hath the life; he that hath not the Son of God hath not the life" (I. v. 10–12).

And this eternal life which we have through the Son differs from our natural life in being a life of holiness. Not even the Apostle Paul, with all his insistence on the ethical contents of faith, goes so far as John does in the entire separation he declares takes place between the believer and sin. The argument is sometimes difficult to follow, as when he tells us, "Whosoever sinneth hath not seen Him, neither knoweth Him. . . . Whosoever is begotten of God doeth no sin" (I. iii. 6–9). "If we say we have no sin, we deceive ourselves" (I. i. 8). It is characteristic of the child of God to endeavour to keep himself pure as his Father in heaven is pure. But if he fall into sin at any time he is not to despair, but to have recourse to his great Advocate

EPISTLES OF JOHN

with the Father, and to His propitiatory sacrifice for forgiveness and cleansing.

It is characteristic of the Apostle of Love that he recognises as the most striking manifestation of the spirit of Christ among the children of God, love to the brethren. No writer has put this more strongly than John does in this Epistle: "He that saith he is in the light, and hateth his brother, is in the darkness until now" (I. ii. 9). "In this the children of God are manifest, and the children of the devil; whosoever doeth not righteousness is not of God, neither he that loveth not his brother" (I. iii. 10). "We know that we have passed out of death into life, because we love the brethren" (I. iii. 14). John, like Paul, sums up his gospel in love: "This is the message which ye heard from the beginning, that we should love one another" (I. iii. 11). "This is His commandment, that we should believe in the name of His Son Jesus Christ, and love one another, even as He gave us commandment" (I. iii. 23).

XIV

SUMMARY OF PAUL'S GOSPEL

WE are now in a position to gather up the results of our examination of the Pauline Epistles, and to form a clear conception of the gospel as Paul was in the habit of presenting it. The conclusion I have sought to establish is, that it was essentially the same gospel as that of the Saviour and His immediate disciples. The view of Christ's person and work is the same as that taken by the writers of the Gospels. It has sometimes been said that the fact that Paul so seldom refers to incidents in the Saviour's life or to the Gospels seems to indicate his ignorance of the Gospels. It is impossible to say when Matthew's Gospel was in the possession of the Church, but it is almost certain that the other three Gospels were not composed till after Paul had written his letters. The Gospel of Mark is generally supposed to contain Peter's reminiscences of the Lord's life. Luke, again, is thought by many to have been largely influenced in his view of the Saviour's life and teaching by his long intercourse with the Apostle

Paul, but we must give him the credit he claims of having consulted the best living authorities for his facts and his reports of Christ's sayings. The absence of direct references to the historic Christ in Paul's writings may be accounted for by the fact that it was the risen and glorified Christ who had revealed Himself to him, and that the main object of his own earlier preaching had been to demonstrate that Jesus was the Messiah of the Jews. At the same time, when we examine in detail Paul's references to the person and work of Christ, we find that they include all the main incidents.

The Gospels represent Jesus as being born into this world from a previous state of existence. He is the Son of God, who was with the Father from the beginning, and by whom all things were created, the source of life and light in this world. From this high estate He voluntarily descends to take upon Him our human nature, to enter upon a condition of service in which He ministered to His fellow-men. The purpose of His advent to the world is declared to be to save sinners. It was that the world through Him might be saved, and His life was devoted to the benefit and the salvation of man. At the same time, the Gospels fix our attention on this great central fact, that His work of salvation was to be accomplished by His death on the Cross and the shedding of His blood for the remission of sin. They are at one, too, in declaring that the death on the Cross did not terminate the life of Jesus. He was raised from the dead, was seen by His disciples to pass into the heavens, where He sat down at the right hand of God the Father, whence He is to appear in the fulness of the time in His glory, to be the judge of the quick and the dead. Now, every one of these leading truths is to be found in Paul's gospel. To him, too, Jesus was the Eternal Son of God, the image of the invisible God, the Creator of all things, in whom were all the treasures of wisdom and knowledge hidden; who of His own free will left His state of glory, emptied Himself is Paul's expression; took upon Him our nature, or, as he puts it, was made flesh, of the seed of David. His condition on earth was one of poverty. He appeared among His fellow-men in the likeness of a servant. The end He contemplated in thus coming to earth was the salvation of sinners, the restoration of man to the family of God. Unquestionably Paul dwells far more in his writings on the means by which Jesus accomplished this salvation. It is the sufferings and death of Jesus he emphasises. His suffering, His crucifixion, His blood, His cross, His sacrifice, the propitiation He made, are the subjects on which He delights to dwell. Wherever he went, or to whatsoever Church he was writing, he made "Jesus Christ and Him crucified" the main theme of his teaching. This theme he presents in every possible light. It is the outcome of the divine love, as well as the satisfaction of the divine justice. It is the propitiation for man's sin, and the example for man in suffering. And certainly

Paul also emphasised the resurrection of Jesus Christ. It was the risen Christ he knew best, and he recognised the importance of this truth to the very existence of the Christian Church. To him Jesus was a living, reigning, and conquering Saviour, who was subduing all things to Himself, and was to appear again in the glory of His Father and of the holy angels to judge the world, to render "vengeance to them that know not God and to them that obey not the gospel of our Lord Jesus Christ, and to be glorified in His saints, and to be marvelled at in all them that believed."[1] It may, indeed, be said that the ideas of representation, substitution, and propitiation are not so prominent in the gospel of Jesus as in that of Paul. True, but the germ of these ideas is there. These truths are in the bud in the Gospels and blossom in the Epistles.

We have seen, then, in what form the gospel is stated by the Evangelists, and in what form it is stated by Paul. We have seen how closely they resemble each other in subject-matter, in style, and often in the very words. Can it then be said that Paul was teaching another gospel? His own language shows that he himself believed that he was preaching and teaching the faith once delivered to the saints, that his gospel was the same as that generally received by the Apostles and the early disciples of Jesus. The gospel of Paul was the gospel of Jesus.

[1] II. Thess. i. 8–10.

www.ingramcontent.com/pod-product-compliance
Lightning Source LLC
Chambersburg PA
CBHW030350170426
43202CB00010B/1323